# *A Course In Miracles*
# In a Nutshell

## Book One

# A Course in Miracles
# *In a Nutshell*


# *Book One*


*"This is reality, and only this.
This is illusion's end.
It is the truth."*
**- *A Course in Miracles***

# Francis M. "Bud" Morris

# *A Course in Miracles In a Nutshell*

## Second Edition

ISBN #978-0-9777219-0-6

Inquiries should be made to
Transformation Publications.

Published by Transformation Publications
5529 E. Harmon Circle
Mesa, AZ 85215
Online at: http://www.budmorris.com

Printed in USA through the publisher's agency,
OPA Publishing,
A division of:
Optimum Performance Associates
Box 1764
Chandler, AZ 85244-1764
E-mail: info@opapublishing.com
Online at: http://www.opapublishing.com

# Table of Contents

*A Course in Miracles* – In a Nutshell

*A Course in Miracles* – In a Nutshell

# Preface

*A* **Course in Miracles in a Nutshell** consists of quotes from *A Course in Miracles,* which is published by the Foundation for Inner Peace. It is intended to introduce the newcomer to *A Course in Miracles*, to explain what the Course teaches, and to provide a source for both the newcomer and the "experienced" Course student for ideas from the Course on selected subjects.

This book was originally intended as an aid for my study group, originating from a list of definitions by Burt Hotchkiss. It gradually expanded over time to its present configuration.

I have added commentary material to a selection of the quotes, which will help to explain the concepts and terms used in the Course.

Grateful appreciation is extended to my wife, Peg Carter, Burt Hotchkiss, Jim and Sally Dunn, Dr. Michael Ryce, my study groups, the Miracle Distribution Center, and to the Course itself for bringing joy and peace into my life. And especially, my gratitude includes Paul McNeese of OPA Publishing for his assistance in preparing this second edition for publication.

# About the Course

*A* ***Course in Miracles*** is a course of study which is read in many countries around the world, having been translated into nine languages with several other translations in process. A Course in Miracles consists of three volumes; *The Text, The Workbook for Students,* and *The Manual for Teachers.* Most of the time, all three of these, in the above order, are contained in one volume. *Note:* The quotes in this book are cross-referenced after each quote with T (*The Text*), WB (*Workbook for Students*), and TM (*Manual for Teachers*), followed by the page number so that, if you desire, you can read more of the material following or preceding the quotation. To complicate matters, a second edition of the Course has been published with additional material as well as page headings and paragraph numbering added which necessarily changed the page numbers from the earlier edition. The page number before the "/" represents the page number from the old edition and the page numbers after it are for the new edition. For example, T25.2/27.3 refers to *The Text.* The quote is on page 25, paragraph 2 (.2) if you are reading in the old edition or in paragraph 3 (.3) of page 27 in the new. Some of the quotes are from the *Song of Prayer,* which is a supplement to the Course. The page number for quotes from the *Song of Prayer* before the slash are from the old book, and behind the slash (example: S-3/IV.6) are from the new edition and indicates the paragraph number. All of these books are available through your local metaphysical bookstore or the Miracle Distribution Center at http://www.miraclecenter.org/.

The goal of the Course is the achievement of inner peace. The *truth* of the world is spiritual, and that which is spiritual cannot be seen with the eyes of the body. The truth is the Presence of God, the Peace of Christ, and the Presence of the Holy Spirit in all situations and all people, whether or not that seems to be the case.

As you read *The Text,* there may be times when you don't

understand what the Course is saying. When this happens, simply be patient and wait until you mature in the principles of the Course. For example, *The Text* consistently speaks on two levels, that of man and that of God. Sometimes this becomes a little confusing. A study group would help with this issue. A list of study groups is available from the Miracles Distribution Center at http://www.miraclecenter.org/. The Course is not to be intellectually analyzed. When you are ready to understand it, the teacher and the understanding will be there. Usually if you have difficulty with a sentence or section, it will be clarified in the next section.

It is recommended that you start the study of the Course with the workbook, one lesson per day. This involves reading the lesson in the morning and evening and keeping the thought with you all day long. The thought for the day is well used as the subject of meditation. Each lesson is very beautiful and transformational, although the first 25–30 lessons have been found to be somewhat challenging by some students. The Preface is important—it relates the history of the origin of the Course. Also, the Introduction to *The Text* and the 50 miracle principles at the beginning of *The Text* are valuable reading. Read in *The Text* and *The Teachers Manual* as you get the opportunity. *The Teachers Manual* is not just for teachers—it is easy to read and clarifies terms and concepts in the Course. Be patient in the way you do the Course, for everyone does it differently and the way they do it is perfect for them. There is no "right" way.

In the Course, the Sons of God consists of all humankind. God is neither masculine nor feminine and His Sons are not referenced according to gender. It consistently references both sexes as "your brother." This causes consternation to some students of the Course in the light of today's sexually "enlightened" state of the world.

*A Course in Miracles* was channeled from Christ. I did not write it! The Course was channeled thorough Dr. Helen Schucman with the assistance of Dr. William Thetford. The Preface of the Course gives details of the history of the Course. Christ is giving you His message today that was so misunderstood in his day and has been continuously misunderstood for many generations since. From the quotes in this book, one gets an insight into Christ's love for God and for humankind and the source of his strength and miracles. In the Course, Christ urges you to remember your Father and your

Father's love for you. He tells how much your Father needs you. He teaches you how to relate to the world, to your brother, and to yourself. He also redefines some biblical terms and concepts.

*A Course in Miracles* is a call to remember your Father who loves you. It is alternatively simple, humorous, and complex. *The Text*, especially, is very profound and cannot be read like a novel. The authority from which the Course comes is apparent in every sentence. Christ's teaching techniques are without flaw, consistent, and totally beautiful. Quotes in this book are a mere sampling of the thousands of beautiful quotes in the Course.

*A Course in Miracles* approaches you and your fellow human beings from a spiritual viewpoint. Both of you are extensions of your Father's Love, and as such, your basic nature is love. No matter what you may have done or been or what your brother may have done or been, your basic nature cannot be altered. The Course speaks of reality from the view of the spiritual nature of all things and all events. You learn through the Course to step back from the drama and trauma of the world to see, not through your physical eyes but through your spiritual eyes, that your growth depends upon the growth of all of your brothers in God and vice-versa. As you see them you see yourself; as you treat them, you treat yourself. In them you find your salvation (healing). You learn how to form a different kind of relationship with all of humankind, with God, with Christ, and with yourself.

*A Course in Miracles* uses terms that are defined differently from the way you may be accustomed. Please refer to the Glossary for selected definitions.

*A Course in Miracles* promotes a way of thinking that helps you to realize that you are not alone, and that you are much greater than you think you are. **You are a miracle; you are the light of the world. YOU ARE AN ANGEL!** Lift your wings and fly!

With Love,

Bud

*A Course in Miracles* — In a Nutshell

# Introduction
## (from A Course in Miracles)

This is a Course in miracles. It is a required Course. Only the time you take it is voluntary. Free will does not mean that you can establish the curriculum. It means only that you can elect what you want to take at a given time. The Course does not aim at teaching the meaning of love, for that is beyond what can be taught. It does aim, however, at removing the blocks to the awareness of love's presence, which is your natural inheritance. The opposite of love is fear, but what is all-encompassing can have no opposite.

This Course can therefore be summed up very simply in this way:

**Nothing real can be threatened.**

**Nothing unreal exists.**

Herein lies the peace of God.

# Favorite Quotes

The next few pages list some of the most powerful quotes from the Course. They have had great meaning for me in my life and I hope you are blessed, also.

*Of yourself you can do nothing, because of yourself you are nothing.*

T135.2/145.7

*You cannot be totally committed sometimes.*

T117.4/127.1

*The goal of the curriculum, regardless of the teacher you choose is "Know thyself." There is nothing else to seek.*

T132.2/142.5

*Arrogance is the denial of love, because love shares and arrogance withholds.*

T178.4/192.4

*Spirit am I, a holy Son of God,*

*Free of all limits, safe and healed and whole,*

*Free to forgive, and free to save the world.*

WB171.1/173.7

*I am the light of the world. That is my only function. That is why I am here.*

WB101.5/102.5

This is who **you** truly are.

*I who am host to God am worthy of Him. He Who established His dwelling place in me created it as He would have it be. It is not needful that I make it ready for Him, but only that I do not interfere with His plan to restore to me my own awareness of my readiness, which is eternal. I need add nothing to His plan. But to receive it, I must be willing not to substitute my own in place of it.*

T356.0/381.5

*You have no problems, though you think you have.*

T506.3/544.3

*There is a light in you which cannot die; whose presence is so holy that the world is sanctified because of you. All things that live bring gifts to you, and offer them in gratitude and gladness at your feet.*

WB287.4/294.4

*The mind is very powerful, and never loses its creative force. It never sleeps. Every instant it is creating. It is hard to recognize that thought and belief combine into a power surge that can literally move mountains.*

T27.1/31.9

*When your mood tells you that you have chosen wrongly, and this is so whenever you are not joyous, then know **this need not be** . . . When you are sad, know **this need not be** . . . When you are anxious, realize that anxiety comes from the capriciousness of the ego, and know **this need not be** . . . While you feel guilty your ego is in command, because only the ego can experience guilt. **This need not be**.*

T57.2, .3, & .4/63.3, .4, & .5

*I am responsible for what I see*
*I choose the feelings I experience and I decide upon the*
*goal I would achieve.*
*And everything that seems to happen to me.*
*I ask for, and receive as I have asked.*

T418.0/448.2

The quote above is hard for many to handle. The idea of taking responsibility for anything in your life is beyond belief to your ego thought system. However, you create your own reality—your mind and thoughts are very powerful. The sum total of human thinking is very powerful. You draw to you the events and people that are in your universe. Don't feel guilty about it, just take action. Ask the Holy Spirit for help, to take it from you, because you are sick and tired of being sick and tired.

*You are altogether irreplaceable in the Mind of God...To accept yourself as God created you cannot be arrogance, because it is the denial of arrogance. To accept your littleness is arrogant, because it means that you believe your evaluation of yourself is truer than God's.*

T167.3/179.10

*Resign now as your own teacher.*

T211.1/227.8

*All things work together for good.*

T59.2/65.1

**All** things—it doesn't say **Some** things. Blessings are there behind every seemingly tragic event in your life. They may not show up for a long time and maybe not ever, but often you can look back over a period of time at a "tragedy" that happened and see the bigger picture and the blessing.

*The truth in you remains as radiant as a star, as pure as light, as innocent as love itself. And you are worthy that your will be done!*

T615.4/662.7

In the Course you find no shades of difference, no grays—just black and white. Here you find no place to have excuses for mistakes. This is not to make you feel guilty or wrong, but an

*A Course in Miracles* – In a Nutshell

opportunity to forgive yourself and ask the Holy Spirit for help, Your creations are defined as those times you extended the Father's love into your life. Your miscreations are those times when you tried to do it by yourself

*I have said that you cannot change your mind by changing your behavior, but I have also said, and many times, that you **can** change your mind.*

T57.2/63.2

*The "devil" is a frightening concept because he seems to be extremely powerful and extremely active. He is perceived as a force in combat with God, battling Him for possession of His creations. The devil deceives by lies, and builds kingdoms in which everything is in direct opposition to God. Yet he attracts men rather than repels them, and they are willing to "sell" him their souls in return for gifts of no real worth. This makes absolutely no sense.*

T44.4/49.2

*The branch that bears no fruit will be cut off and will wither away. Be glad! The light will shine from the true Foundation of life, and your own thought system will stand corrected . . . Your kingdom is not of this world because it was given you from beyond this world.*

T46.1/51.6

*What profiteth it a man if he gain the whole world and lose his own soul? If you listen to the wrong voice you have lost sight of your soul. You cannot lose it, but you can not know it. It is therefore "lost" to you until you choose right.*

T70.2/76.7

*"'Vengeance is mine,' sayeth the Lord" is easily reinterpreted if you remember that ideas increase only by being shared. The statement emphasizes that vengeance cannot be shared. Give it therefore to the Holy Spirit, Who will undo it in you because it does not belong in your mind, which is part of God.*

T80.5/87.7

Ideas are spiritual in nature. They are not like a book, for example. When you give away a book, it is gone; it is not in your hands or in your possession anymore. The Course teaches that an idea gains in strength when it is given away. You, by giving an idea away, have it reinforced in yourself. You teach what you want to learn.

*Listen to the story of the prodigal son, and learn what God's treasure is and yours: The son of a loving father left his home and thought he had squandered everything for nothing of any value, although he had not understood its worthlessness at the time. He was ashamed to return to his father, because he thought he had hurt him. Yet when he came home the father welcomed him with joy, because the son himself was his father's treasure. He wanted nothing else.*

T138.3 & .4/148.4, .5

You are your Father's only treasure!

*Ultimately, every member of the family of God must return. The miracle calls him to return because it blesses and honors him, even though he may be absent in spirit. "God is not mocked" is not a warning but a reassurance. God* **would** *be mocked if any of His creations lacked holiness. The creation is whole, and the mark of wholeness is holiness. Miracles are affirmations of Sonship, which is a state of completion and abundance.*

T10.3/13.4

*Rejoice, then, that of yourself you can do nothing.* **You** *are not* **of** *yourself.*

T141.2/152.6

*Have you really considered how many opportunities you have had to gladden yourself, and how many of them you have refused? There is no limit to the power of a Son of God, but he can limit the expression of his power as much as he chooses.*

T58.2/64.8

*A Course in Miracles* – In a Nutshell

# Abundance

Abundance is more than just money, property, or belongings. True abundance originates in the heart. Things of this world are merely physical and as is stated in the Bible, can be stolen, decayed, or corrupted. The qualities of God, such as Love and Peace, are in the abundant heart and they can never be lost nor corrupted in any way.

> *The abundance of Christ is the natural result of choosing to follow Him.*
>
> T10.5/13.6

> *You were given everything when you were created just as everyone was.*
>
> T9.1/11.3

You are created in the image of God, a Child of God.

> *Ask and it shall be given you, because it has already **been** given just as everyone was.*
>
> T131.2/141.1

> *Truth is always abundant. Those who perceive and acknowledge that they have everything have no needs of any kind.*
>
> T9.1/11.3

> *Poverty is of the ego, and never of God.*
>
> T206.1/221.4

> *Give, therefore, of your abundance, and teach your brothers theirs. Do not share their illusions of scarcity, or you will perceive yourself as lacking.*
>
> T119.2/128.7

*Only those who have a real and lasting sense of abundance can be truly charitable.*

T52.2/58.6

*Would God consent to let His Son remain forever starved by his denial of the nourishment he needs to live? Abundance dwells in him, and deprivation cannot cut him off from God's sustaining Love and from his home.*

WB306.7/314.6

*This tiny spot of sin that stands between you and your brother still is holding back the happy opening of Heaven's gate. How little is the hindrance that withholds the wealth of Heaven from you. And how great will be the joy in Heaven when you join the mighty chorus to the Love of God!*

T510.5/549.6

# Anger

Anger is a form of insanity, but nonetheless is a valid feeling. The lesson in anger is to understand as soon as possible the true reason for the feeling and to give it over to the Holy Spirit for healing. Anger can be a great motivator, but remember that all anger is based in fear.

> *All anger is nothing more than an attempt to make someone feel guilty.*
>
> T297.1/319.10

This is a quote with major implications! Be aware of every angry feeling that you have through the day and at the time that the feeling is happening, ask yourself who you are trying to make feel guilty.

> *Anger cannot occur unless you believe that you have been attacked, that your attack is justified in return, and that you are in no way responsible for it.*
>
> T84.1/91.1

> *Therefore, hold no one prisoner. Release instead of bind, for thus are you made free. The way is simple. Every time you feel a stab of anger, realize you hold a sword above your head. And it will fall or be averted as you choose to be condemned or free. Thus does each one who seems to tempt you to be angry represent your savior from the prison house of death. And so you owe him thanks instead of pain.*
>
> WB356.3/366.9

> *Today we practice differently, and take a stand against our anger, that our fears may disappear and offer room to love. Here is salvation in the simple words in which we practice with today's idea. Here is the answer to temptation, which can never fail to welcome*

*in the Christ where fear and anger had prevailed before. Here is Atonement made complete, the world passed safely by and Heaven now restored. Here is the answer of the Voice for God.*

WB297.1/304.1

*How is this quiet found? No one can fail to find it who but seeks out its conditions. God's peace can never come where anger is, for anger must deny that peace exists. Who sees anger as justified in any way or any circumstance proclaims that peace is meaningless, and must believe that it cannot exist. In this condition, peace cannot be found.*

TM49.3/51.3

# Atonement

Atonement is defined in the Course as the undoing of error. The atonement is usually thought of as something that God grants you in forgiveness for your "sins." Another way of looking at Atonement is At-one-ment, at one with God, with Spirit. When you recognize your oneness with God, you simultaneously recognize that your "sins" were never real and that you are healed.

> When the Atonement has been completed, all talents will be shared by all the Sons of God. God is not partial. All His children have His total Love, and all His gifts are freely given to everyone alike. "Except ye become as little children" means that unless you fully recognize your complete dependence on God, you cannot know the real power of the Son in his true relationship with the Father.
>
> T10.2/12.3

The Atonement is defined as the removal of guilt which results in the "undoing of error"—a healing, with a simultaneous release of fear.

> The Atonement is a total commitment. You may still think this is associated with loss, a mistake all the separated Sons of God make in one way or another. It is hard to believe a defense that cannot attack is the best defense. This is what is meant by "the meek shall inherit the earth." They will literally take it over because of their strength...The miracle turns the defense of Atonement to your real protection, and as you become more and more secure you assume your natural talent of protecting others, knowing yourself as both a brother and a Son.
>
> T17.2/20.7

People who are religious or spiritual are considered as "wimps" by some. Exactly the opposite is true. Consider the Christians and the lions, for example. It took a lot of strength for a person to stand there and face death. It took a lot of faith. It takes a lot of faith and strength to be a Jew in the face of prejudices and abuses towards them. Look at all that Gandhi accomplished in the face of the British. When you have the Force of the Universe, God, truly in your consciousness, your strength is that of legions. The Course speaks of your defenselessness, that in your defenselessness your safety lies. If you defend, you are attacked; that is, you attract attack with your defense.

*Healing and Atonement are not related; they are identical. There is no order of difficulty in miracles because there are no degrees of Atonement. It is the one complete concept possible in this world, because it is the source of a wholly unified perception. Partial Atonement is a meaningless idea, just as special areas of hell in Heaven are inconceivable. Accept Atonement and you are healed. Atonement is the Word of God.*

TM53.1/55.1

*The Atonement does not make holy. You were created holy.*

T270.3/291.1

*Steps in process of accepting the Atonement as the remedy of error:*

*1. Know first that this (error) is fear.*

*2. Fear arises from lack of love.*

*3. The only remedy for lack of love is perfect love.*

*4. Perfect love is the Atonement.*

T26.2/30.7

*The Atonement principle is love and the Atonement is an act of love.* (paraphrased)

T16.3/19.4

*"The wicked shall perish" becomes a statement of Atonement, if the word "perish" is understood as "be undone."*

T80.7/87.9

*If a mind perceives without love, it perceives an empty shell and is unaware of the spirit within. But the Atonement restores spirit to its proper place. The mind that serves spirit is invulnerable.*

T8.0/11.2

*Our emphasis is now on healing. The miracle is the means, the Atonement is the principle, and healing is the result. To speak of "a miracle of healing" is to combine two orders of reality inappropriately. Healing is not a miracle. The Atonement, or the final miracle, is a remedy and any type of healing is a result. The kind of error to which Atonement is applied is irrelevant. All healing is essentially the release from fear.*

T19.2/23.1

*Today accept Atonement, not to change reality, but merely to accept the truth about yourself, and go your way rejoicing in the endless Love of God.*

WB261.4/268.10

# Attack Thoughts

Your judgments towards others are attack thoughts. Since there is only one Son of God, these attack thoughts are directed at yourself.

> *Because your attack thoughts will be projected, you will fear attack. And if you fear attack, you must believe that you are not invulnerable. Attack thoughts therefore make you vulnerable in your own mind, which is where the attack thoughts are. Attack thoughts and invulnerability cannot be accepted together. They contradict each other.*
>
> WB40.2/40.2

> *I can escape from this world by giving up attack thoughts. Herein lies salvation, and nowhere else. Without attack thoughts I could not see a world of attack. As forgiveness allows love to return to my awareness, I will see a world peace and safety and joy. And it is this I choose to see, in place of what I look on now.*
>
> WB89.3/90.3

You can escape from the insanity in this world through giving up attack thoughts.

> *The world I see is hardly the representation of loving thoughts. It is a picture of attack on everything by everything. It is anything but a reflection of the Love of God and the Love of His Son. It is my own attack thoughts that give rise to this picture. My loving thoughts will save me from this perception of the world, and give me the peace God intended me to have.*
>
> WB89.2/90.2

# The Body

The physical body that you inhabit at present is the device the ego uses for blocking you from God. You are so attached to the body and bodily functions that your attention is distracted from your spiritual search. The physical universe provides a similar distraction with all its busy-ness. Be ye *in* the body (world) but not *of* it! Be glad that you can see the body for the vehicle that it is. Take care of it, but don't worship it.

*The body is merely part of your experience in the physical world. Its abilities can be and frequently are over-evaluated. However, it is almost impossible to deny its existence in this world.*

T20.1/23.3

*The body is outside you, and but seems to surround you, shutting you off from others and keeping you apart from them, and them from you. It is not there. There is no barrier between God and His Son, nor can His Son be separated from Himself except in illusions.*

T360.4/386.9

*You are not limited by the body, and thought cannot be made flesh. Yet mind can be manifested through the body if it goes beyond it and does not interpret it as limitation. Whenever you see another as limited to or by the body, you are imposing this limit on yourself.*

T143.1/154.14

# Brotherhood

Your brother and yourself are one Son of the one God. You are all created by God and imbued with His Life Force. You are your brothers' keeper. The brotherhood consists of individuals— many fingers originating from one Hand as God created the One Son in multiplicity—different bodies, but one Spirit.

In the Course, the Sons of God consists of all humankind. God is neither masculine nor feminine and His Sons are not referenced according to gender. It consistently references both sexes as "your brother." This causes consternation to some students of the Course in the light of today's sexually "enlightened" state of the world.

> When you meet anyone, remember it is a holy encounter. As you see him, you will see yourself. As you treat him you will treat yourself. As you think of him, you will think of yourself. Never forget this, for in him, you will find yourself or lose yourself.
>
> T132.1/142.4

> Remember that it does not matter where in the Sonship He is accepted. He is always accepted for all, and when your mind receives Him the remembrance of Him awakens throughout the Sonship. Heal your brothers simply by accepting God for them. Your minds are not separate, and God has only one channel for healing because He has but one Son.
>
> T171.2/184.2

> My holy brother, I would enter into all your relationships, and step between you and your fantasies. Let my relationship to you be real to you, and let me bring reality to your perception of your brothers.
>
> T333.1/357.10

*A Course in Miracles* – In a Nutshell

15

*When you feel the holiness of your relationship is threatened by anything, stop instantly and offer the Holy Spirit your willingness, in spite of fear, to let Him exchange this instant for the holy one that you would rather have. He will never fail in this...Whoever is saner at the time the threat is perceived should remember how deep is his indebtedness to the other and how much gratitude is due him, and be glad that he can pay his debt by bringing happiness to both.*

T358.1/384.6

*Condemn* (your brother) *not by seeing him within the rotting prison where he sees himself. It is your special function to ensure the door be opened, that he may come forth to shine on you, and give you back the gift of freedom by receiving it of you.*

T505.4/544.8

*You think you hold against your brother what he has done to you. But what you really blame him for is what* **you** *did to* **him.**

T344.2/369.8

You blame him for **your** guilt.

*You groped but feebly in the dust and found your brother's hand, uncertain whether to let it go or to take hold on life so long forgotten. Strengthen your hold and raise your eyes unto your strong companion, in whom the meaning of your freedom lies. He seemed to be crucified beside you. And yet his holiness remained untouched and perfect, and with him beside you, you shall this day enter with him to Paradise, and know the peace of God.*

T402.0/431.9

Turning the other cheek can also be interpreted as seeing from a different viewpoint, or with new perception. When the Course says your brother cannot hurt you, it doesn't make sense, until you realize that you are not your body. You have identified with the body all of your life, but you are truly an idea in the Mind of God. You are a spiritual being having a physical experience.

*The Bible says that you should go with a brother twice*

*as far as he asks. It certainly does not suggest that you set him back on his journey. Devotion to a brother cannot set you back either. It can lead only to mutual progress.*

T47.1/52.1

*This week (Easter) begins with palms and ends with lilies, the white and holy sign the Son of God is innocent. Let no dark sign of crucifixion intervene between the journey and its purpose; between the acceptance of the truth and its expression. This week we celebrate life, not death. And we honor the perfect purity of the Son of God, and not his sins. Offer your brother the gift of lilies, not the crown of thorns; the gift of love and not the "gift" of fear. You stand beside your brother, thorns in one hand and lilies in the other, uncertain which to give. Join now with me and throw away the thorns, offering the lilies to replace them.*

T396.2 & .4/425.2 & .4

*You cannot be hurt, and do not want to show your brother anything except your wholeness. Show him that he cannot hurt you and hold nothing against him, or you hold it against yourself. This is the meaning of "turning the other cheek."*

T75.2/82.4

# Christit

The personal pronouns used in the quotes in this section reflect the author of the Course—Christ. The Course is Christ's effort to explain his position in God's Plan. The life of Christ is an example of how you are to live your life in Love and everlasting kindness and freedom. I honor Christ as my elder brother and way-shower, not as the only son of God. Christ was a man who lived his divinity; Spirit moved through him unceasingly.

*The sight of Christ is all there is to see. The song of Christ is all there is to hear. The hand of Christ is all there is to hold. There is no journey but to walk with Him.*

T474.4/510.7

*"No man cometh unto the Father but by me" does not mean that I am in any way separate or different from you except in time, and time does not really exist. The statement is more meaningful in terms of a vertical rather than a horizontal axis. You stand below me and I stand below God. In the process of "rising up," I am higher because without me the distance between God and man would be too great for you to encompass. I bridge the distance as an elder brother to you on the one hand, and as a Son of God on the other. My devotion to my brothers has placed me in charge of the Sonship, which I render complete because I share it. This may appear to contradict the statement "I and my Father are one," but there are two parts to the statement in recognition that the Father is greater.*

T5.3/7.4

*Christ is at God's Altar, waiting to welcome His Son. But come wholly without condemnation, for otherwise you will believe that the door is barred and you cannot enter. The door is not barred, and it is impossible that you cannot enter the place where God would have you be...You can refuse to enter, but you cannot bar the door that Christ holds open. Come unto me who holds it open for you, for while I live it cannot be shut, and I live forever.*

T187.2/201.6

*I will never leave or forsake you, because to forsake you would be to forsake myself and God Who created me.*

T76.1/82.6

*Every child of God is one in Christ, for his being is in Christ as Christ's is in God. Christ's Love for you is His Love for His Father, which He knows because He knows His Father's Love for Him. When the Holy Spirit has at last led you to Christ at the altar to His Father, perception fuses into knowledge because perception has become so holy that its transfer to holiness is merely its natural extension.*

T213.1/229.1

*When I said, "I am with you always," I meant it literally. I am not absent to anyone in any situation. Because I am always with you, you are the way, the truth and the life. You did not make this power, any more than I did.*

T107.3/116.1

*I am come as a light into a world that does deny itself everything . . . I said that I am with you always, even unto the end of the world. That is why I am the light of the world. If I am with you in the loneliness of the world, the loneliness is gone.*

T133.4/144.2

*As God sent me to you so will I send you to others. And I will go to them with you, so we can teach them peace and union.*

T134.1/144.3

*When you are tempted by the wrong voice, call on me to remind you how to heal by sharing my decision and making it stronger. As we share this goal, we increase its power to attract the whole Sonship, and to bring it back into the oneness in which it was created. Remember that "yoke" means "join together," and "burden" means "message." Let us restate "My yoke is easy and my burden light" in this way; "Let us join together, for my message is Light."*

T71.2/77.11

*The sign of Christmas is a star, a light in darkness. See it not outside yourself, but shining in the Heaven within, and accept it as the sign the time of Christ has come. He comes demanding nothing. No sacrifice of any kind, of anyone, is asked by Him.*

T304.2/327.2

*Holy child of God, when will you learn that only holiness can content you and give you peace? . . . I would but teach you what is yours, so that together we can replace the shabby littleness that binds the host of God to guilt and weakness with the glad awareness of the glory that is in him. My birth in you is your awakening to grandeur. Welcome me not into a manger, but into the altar to holiness, where holiness abides in perfect peace. My Kingdom is not of this world because it is in you. And you are of your Father.*

T287.1/308.9

*A little while and you will see me, for I am not hidden because **you** are hiding. I will awaken you as surely as I awakened myself, for I awoke for you. In my resurrection is your release.*

T204.2/219.7

*My brothers slept during the so-called "agony in the garden," but I could not be angry with them because I knew I could not be abandoned.*

T86.2/93.7

*I elected, for your sake and mine, to demonstrate that*

*the most outrageous assault, as judged by the ego, does not matter. As the world judges these things, but not as God knows them, I was betrayed, abandoned, beaten, torn, and finally killed. It was clear that this was only because of the projection of others onto me, since I had not harmed anyone and had healed many.*

T86.2/93.9

The entry above explains Christ's perception during his crucifixion. Whenever you feel attacked, you have the choice to react in love towards your attackers. Forgive them, for they know not what they do.

*I have been correctly referred to as "the lamb of God who taketh away the sins of the world," but those who represent the lamb as bloodstained do not understand the meaning of the symbol. Correctly understood, it is a very simple symbol that speaks of my innocence. The lion and the lamb lying down together symbolize that strength and innocence are not in conflict, but naturally live in peace.*

T33.2 & .3/37.5 & .6

*I was a man who remembered spirit and its knowledge. As a man I did not attempt to counteract error with knowledge, but to correct error from the bottom up. I demonstrated both the powerlessness of the body and the power of the mind. By uniting my will with that of my Creator, I naturally remembered spirit and its real purpose. I cannot unite your will with God's for you, but I can erase all misperceptions from your mind if you will bring it under my guidance. Only your misperceptions stand in your way. Without them your choice is certain . . . I cannot choose for you, but I can help you make your own right choice. "Many are called but few are chosen" should be, "All are called but few choose to listen." Therefore, they do not choose right. The "chosen ones" are merely those who choose right sooner.*

T39.1/43.7

When you seem to be in trouble, choose to listen to the call of the Holy Spirit. When you relax, go within, and become peaceful, the answer to your "problems" can be heard. When you are in the midst of your trauma and drama, on the "battlefield" of a situation, the "still, small voice" is ever available.

*The Bible enjoins you to be perfect, to heal all errors, to take no thought of the body as separate and to accomplish all things in my name. This is not my name alone, for ours is a shared identification. The Name of God's Son is one, and you are enjoined to do the works of love because we share this oneness.*

T147.4/159.7

*I do not bring God's message with deception, and you will learn this as you learn that you always receive as much as you accept. You could accept peace now for everyone, and offer them perfect freedom from all illusions because you heard His Voice. But have no other gods before Him or you will not hear. God is not jealous of the gods you make, but you are.*

T172.4/186.8

*In this world you need not have tribulation because I have overcome the world. That is why you should be of good cheer.*

T51.0/56.13

# Conflict

Conflict is part of the illusion, part of the dream. All of your conflicts in your families, in your work, in your going from place to place, is not of God, for God knows not of conflict. The choice between peace and conflict may be obvious, but often the habit of conflict overwhelms peaceful desires. Attack often is an automatic reaction that is regretted later.

> The real conflict you experience, then, is between the ego's idle wishes and the Will of God, which you share. Can this be a real conflict?
>
> T189.1/203.5

> Pain is not of Him, for He knows no attack and His peace surrounds you silently. God is very quiet, for there is no conflict in Him. Conflict is the root of all evil, for being blind it does not see whom it attacks. Yet it always attacks the Son of God, and the Son of God is you.
>
> T184.2/198.1

> There **is** no conflict in the choice between truth and illusion. Seen in these terms, no one would hesitate. But conflict enters the instant the choice seems to be one between illusions, but this choice does not matter. Where one choice is as dangerous as the other, the decision must be one of despair.
>
> T315.1/338.5

> See how the conflict of illusions disappears when it is brought to truth! For it seems real only as long as it is seen as war between conflicting truths; the conqueror to be the truer, the more real, and the vanquisher of the illusion that was less real, made an illusion by defeat. Thus, conflict is the choice between illusions, one to be

*crowned as real, the other vanquished and despised. Here will the Father never be remembered. Yet no illusion can invade His home and drive Him out of what He loves forever. And what He loves must be forever quiet and at peace **because** it is His home.*

T454.2/488.9

# Creation

There is a definite distinction in the Course between "make" and "create." You make with the ego, but you create with God. Your creations are your loving thoughts. God created you in His Image—whole, perfect, complete, and free.

> *You have lost the knowledge that you yourself are a miracle of God. Creation is your Source and your only real function.*
>
> T40.3/45.6

> *Because of your likeness to your Creator you are creative.*
>
> T14.1/17.1

> *Child of God, you were created to create the good, the beautiful and the holy. Do not forget this. The Love of God, for a little while, must still be expressed through one body to another, because vision is still so dim.*
>
> T12.3/15.2

> *The statement "God created man in his own image and likeness" needs reinterpretation. "Image" can be understood as "thought," and "likeness" as "of a like quality." God did create spirit in His Own Thought and of a quality like to His Own. There is nothing else.*
>
> T40.4/45.7

The Course consistently maintains that this world is but an illusion—created by and maintained by you. God does not recognize it. He did not create it. He holds you as His beautiful Son, who is still as he was created in the likeness of God.

> *Out of your natural environment you may well ask, "What is truth?" since truth is the environment by which and for which you were created. You do not*

*know yourself, because you do not know your Creator. You do not know your creations because you do not know your brothers, who created them with you. I have already said that only the whole Sonship is worthy to be co-creator with God, because only the whole Sonship can create like Him. Whenever you heal a brother by recognizing his worth, you are acknowledging his power to create and yours. He cannot have lost what you recognize, and you must have the glory you see in him. He is a co-creator with God with you. Deny his creative power, and you are denying yours and that of God Who created you.*

T127.3/137.6

*Everyone experiences fear. Yet it would take very little right thinking to realize why fear occurs. Few appreciate the real power of the mind, and no one remains fully aware of it all the time. However, if you hope to spare yourself from fear there are some things you must realize, and realize fully. The mind is very powerful, and never loses its creative force. It never sleeps. Every instant it is creating. It is hard to recognize that thought and belief combine into a power surge that can literally move mountains. It appears at first glance that to believe such power about yourself is arrogant, but that is not the real reason you do not believe it. You prefer to believe that your thoughts cannot exert real influence because you are actually afraid of them.*

T27.1/31.9

# Crucifixion

Jesus in the Course reinterprets the meaning of persecution and the crucifixion. You on this physical plane could consider yourself persecuted, attacked, and crucified in many ways. Look at the events in your life and your relationships with different eyes; reinterpret them from the points of view espoused below.

*The message of the crucifixion is perfectly clear: "Teach only love, for that is what you are."*

*If you interpret the crucifixion in any other way, you are using it as a weapon for assault rather than as the call for peace for which it was intended. The Apostles often misunderstood it, and for the same reason that anyone misunderstands it. Their own imperfect love made them vulnerable to projection, and out of their own fear they spoke of the "wrath of God" as His retaliatory weapon. Nor could they speak of the crucifixion entirely without anger, because their sense of guilt had made them angry.*

*These are some of the examples of upside-down thinking in the New Testament, although its gospel is really only the message of love. If the Apostles had not felt guilty, they never could have quoted me as saying, "I came not to bring peace but a sword." This is clearly the opposite of everything I taught. Nor could they have described my reactions to Judas as they did, if they had really understood me. I could not have said, "Betrayest thou the Son of Man with a kiss?" unless I believed in betrayal. The whole message of the crucifixion was simply that I did not. The "punishment" I was said to have called forth upon Judas was a similar mistake. Judas was my brother and a Son of God, as much a part of the Sonship as myself. Was it likely that I would condemn him when I was ready to demonstrate that condemnation is impossible? As you read the teachings of the Apostles, remember that I told them myself that there was much they would understand later, because they were not wholly ready to follow me at the time.*

T87.2 & .3 & .4/94.13 & .14 & .15

*Nothing can prevail against a Son of God who commends his spirit into the Hands of his Father. By doing this, the mind awakens from its sleep and remembers its Creator. All sense of separation disappears. The Son of God is part of the Holy Trinity, but the Trinity Itself is one.*

T35.1/39.5

If you relate so closely to bodies, both yours and others, then they become a major tool of your separation from God. Your resulting guilt, blame, and shame for this separation becomes a major causal factor for making more of a mess of your life.

*You can speak from the spirit or from the ego, as you choose. If you speak from spirit you have chosen to "Be still and know that I am God."*

*Do not embark on useless journeys, because they are indeed in vain . . .*

*The journey to the cross should be the last "useless journey." Do not dwell upon it, but dismiss it as accomplished. If you can accept it as your own last useless journey, you are also free to join my resurrection...Do not make the pathetic error of "clinging to the old rugged cross." The only message of the crucifixion is that you can overcome the cross. Until then you are free to crucify yourself as often as you choose. This is not the Gospel I intended to offer you. We have another journey to undertake, and if you will read these lessons carefully they will help prepare you to undertake it.*

T47.2 & .3/52.2 & .3

The empty cross is a symbol of eternal life, the resurrection, the promise of God. It is also a reflection of the fact that you can choose to remove yourself from the cross and refrain from crucifying and persecuting yourself at any moment.

*You will not find peace until you have removed the nails from the hands of God's Son, and taken the last thorn from his forehead. The Love of God surrounds His Son whom the god of crucifixion condemns. Teach not that I died in vain. Teach rather that I did not die by demonstrating that I live in you. For the undoing of the crucifixion of God's Son is the work of the redemption, in which everyone has a part of equal value. God does not judge His guiltless Son. Having given Himself to him, how could it be otherwise?*

T193.4/208.7

# Death

Christ's major message in the Bible and the Course is that death is not to be feared. Death is but a transition from the physical to the spiritual, a release from the restrictions of the physical body. When death is feared, death becomes a painful experience. When it is not feared, it becomes a loving and peaceful experience, merely a release and taking on a new identity.

> *This is what death should be; a quiet choice, made joyfully and with a sense of peace, because the body has been kindly used to help the Son of God along the way he goes to God. We thank the body, then, for all the service it has given us. But we are thankful too, the need is done to walk the world of limits, and to reach the Christ in hidden forms and clearly seen at most in lovely flashes. Now we can behold Him without blinders, in the light that we have earned to look upon again.*

> *We call it death, but it is liberty. It does not come in forms that seem to be thrust down in pain upon unwilling flesh, but as a gentle welcome to release. If there has been true healing, this can be the form in which death comes when it is time to rest a while from labor gladly done and gladly ended. Now we go in peace to freer air and gentler climate, where it is not hard to see the gifts we gave were saved for us. For Christ is clearer now; His Vision more sustained in us; His Voice, the Word of God, more certainly our own.*
>
> Song of Prayer 16/ S–3.II.2

This quote from *Song of Prayer* brings great peace to the concept of death.

*. . . nothing is accomplished through death, because death is nothing. Everything is accomplished through life, and life is of the mind and in the mind. The body neither lives nor dies, because it cannot contain you who are life.*

T96.4/104.1

*God, Who created neither sin nor death, wills not that you be bound by them.*

T389.1/417.3

*The Holy Spirit guides you into life eternal, but you must relinquish your investment in death, or you will not see life, though it is all around you.*

T209.2/224.7

# Decisions

The Course constantly puts you at choice between ego and Holy Spirit, between murder and love, and between peace and chaos. You have the power to choose, and choose you constantly do. Would you rather be right or happy? Spend time each morning with Holy Spirit and ask Him for help in choosing happiness.

*"Would you be hostage to the ego or host to God?" Let this question be asked you by the Holy Spirit every time you make a decision. For every decision you make does answer this, and invites sorrow or joy accordingly. When God gave Himself to you in your creation, He established you as host to Him forever. He has not left you, and you have not left Him. All your attempts to deny His magnitude, and make His Son hostage to the ego, cannot make little whom God has joined with Him. Every decision you make is for Heaven or for hell, and brings you the awareness of what you decided for.*

T286.1/307.5

*Whenever you choose to make decisions for yourself you are thinking destructively, and the decision will be wrong. It will hurt you because of the concept of decision that led to it. It is not true that you can make decisions by yourself or for yourself alone. No thought of God's Son can be separate or isolated in its effects. Every decision is made for the whole Sonship, directed in and out, and influencing a constellation larger than anything you ever dreamed of.*

T256.5/276.9

*My decision cannot overcome yours, because yours is as powerful as mine. If it were not so the Sons of God would be unequal. All things are possible through our joint decision, but mine alone cannot help you. Your will is as free as mine, and God Himself would not go against it. I cannot will what God does not will. I can offer my strength to make yours invincible, but I cannot oppose your decision without competing with it and thereby violating God's Will for you.*

T134.3/145.5

# Depression

Depression is anger turned inward; it is a powerful emotion which tends to constantly pull one down into the depths of despair. If you suffer from depression, remember that it is not a natural state and that depression is a lie—it is not your truth. One's natural state is peace, love, and joy, so these are hidden below the feelings of depression. Returning to that natural state might start with small steps that eventually lead through the fear that brought depression, but it can be done. The Workbook Lessons in the Course for a year would be very helpful.

> *Depression comes from a sense of being deprived of something you want and do not have. Remember that you are deprived of nothing except by your own decisions, and then decide otherwise.*
>
> T57.3/63.3

> *Depression means that you have forsworn God. Many are afraid of blasphemy, but they do not understand what it means. They do not realize that to deny God is to deny their own Identity, and in this sense the wages of sin* **is** *death. The sense is very literal; denial of life perceives its opposite, as all forms of denial replace what is with what is not. No one can really do this, but that you can think you can and believe you have is beyond dispute.*
>
> T175.4/189.5

> *Depression is isolation, and so it could not have been created.*
>
> T176.4/190.5

# Dreams

In the Course, you are taught to see and hear, not with your eyes and ears, but through your Spirit. According to the Course, the life you lead is characterized as a dream, in which you see nightmares. These nightmares take many forms—debts, divorces, alcohol, drugs, food, conflicts with people, war, and death—anything which directs your thoughts away from Spirit. Become more conscious of your spiritual truth and your energy attracts the "bad" things into your life to a lesser extent. Become more aware of your true strength and values, those that come from the spiritual side of you, from God. You have wonderful teachers and guides in this, the Christ and the Holy Spirit. Be still and tune into the still, small voice.

*Never forget this; it is you who are God's Son, and as you choose to be to Him so are you to yourself, and God to you. Come unto Me, My children, once again, without such twisted thoughts upon your hearts. You still are holy with the Holiness which fathered you in perfect sinlessness, and still surrounds you with the Arms of Peace. Dream now of healing. Then arise and lay all dreaming down forever. You are he your Father loves, who never left his home, nor wandered in a savage world with feet that bleed, and with a heavy heart made hard against the love that is the truth in you. Give all your dreams to Christ and let Him be your Guide to healing, leading you in prayer beyond the sorry reaches of the world.*

Song of Prayer 19/S–3.IV.6

*Yet the instant you awaken you realize that everything that seemed to happen in the dream did not happen at all...Is it not possible that you merely shifted from one dream to another, without really waking?*

T169.1/182.2

*A Course in Miracles — In a Nutshell*

*Happy dreams come true, not because they are dreams, but only because they are happy. And so they must be loving. Their message is, "Thy Will be done," and not, "I want it otherwise."*

T357.4/383.4

Attempting to control your life is one of your greatest mistakes. If you wish to make God laugh, let Him know that you (ego) are in charge! Live each moment in conscious awareness and as soon as you realize you are in fear or pain, recognize that, at that moment, you are depending on your own strength, and not the strength of the Holy Spirit within you. Turn all your "problems" over to Him.

*He comes for Me and speaks My Word to you. I would recall My weary Son to Me from dreams of malice to the sweet embrace of everlasting Love and perfect peace.*

*Help Me to wake My children from the dream of retribution and a little life beset with fear, that ends so soon it might as well have never been.*

Song of Prayer 20/ S–3.IV.7

*. . . the Bible says that a deep sleep fell upon Adam, and nowhere is there reference to his waking up. The world has not yet experienced any comprehensive re-awakening or rebirth.*

*Only after the deep sleep fell upon Adam could he experience nightmares.*

T14.7 & .8/17.3 & .4

Awaken now! It is too easy to go unconscious, to get caught up in the drama and trauma of the world. Arise from your bed of thorns to God's Love.

*You recognize from your own experience that what you see in dreams you think is real while you are asleep.*

T169.1/182.2

# Easter

Easter is a time when people throng to churches all over the world to remember Christ and his "sacrifice." Christ denies sacrifice. He says in the Course that the world saw him as persecuted, betrayed, and killed, but he did not see it that way. The Son of God is not dead. He lives within us. Do not make the mistake of clinging to the old rugged cross—the world needs the wood! Do not crucify yourself—love yourself as God loves you.

*This Easter I would have the gift of your forgiveness offered by you to me, and returned by me to you. We cannot be united in crucifixion and in death. Nor can the resurrection be complete till your forgiveness rests on Christ, along with mine.*

T396.2/425.2

*Easter is not the celebration of the **cost** of sin, but of its **end**. If you see glimpses of the face of Christ behind the veil, looking between the snow-white petals of the lilies you have received and given as your gift, you will behold your brother's face and recognize it. I was a stranger and you took me in, not knowing who I was. Yet for your gift of lilies you will know. In your forgiveness of this stranger, alien to you and yet your ancient Friend, lies his release and your redemption with him. The time of Easter is a time of joy, and not of mourning. Look on your risen Friend, and celebrate his holiness along with me. For Easter is the time of your salvation, along with mine.*

T396.4/425.4

*The song of Easter is the glad refrain the Son of God was never crucified. Let us lift up our eyes together, not in fear but faith. And there will be no fear in us, for in our vision will be no illusions; only a pathway to the open door of Heaven, the home we share in quietness and where we live in gentleness and peace, as one together.*

T398.4/427.8

*This week (Easter) begins with palms and ends with lilies, the white and holy sign the Son of God is innocent. Let no dark sign of crucifixion intervene between the journey and its purpose; between the acceptance of the truth and its expression. This week we celebrate life, not death. And we honor the perfect purity of the Son of God, and not his sins. Offer your brother the gift of lilies, not the crown of thorns; the gift of love and not the "gift" of fear. You stand beside your brother, thorns in one hand and lilies in the other, uncertain which to give. Join now with me and throw away the thorns, offering the lilies to replace them.*

T396.2 & .4/425.2 & .4

# Ego

A h, the ego! That dastardly villain upon which the Course spends so much ink! Some have compared the ego to the devil; the Course would have you know that your ego is, along with the body, and the world, attempting to keep you separated from God. The ego is nothing but a part of your thought system, which would set you apart, "special," and above other people. Don't place it outside yourself. The ego takes delight in turning you away from spiritual seeking in any form. It can use anything as an idol, a substitute for God. When you grow spiritually, you become aware of the ego's existence and its aptitude for directing your search for fulfillment outside of yourself rather than within. Do not try to destroy the ego, but just to become more and more aware of it. (See the Laws of Chaos section later in this book.)

> *The ego is idolatry; the sign of limited and separated self, born in a body, doomed to suffer and to end its life in death.*
>
> WB457.1/467.1

> *The ego is a contradiction. Your self and God's Self **are** in opposition. They are opposed in source, in direction and in outcome. They are fundamentally irreconcilable, because spirit cannot perceive and the ego cannot know.*
>
> T48.1/53.3

> *The ego is nothing more than a part of your belief about yourself.*
>
> T61.1/67.1

> *Everyone makes an ego or a self for himself, which is subject to enormous variation because of its instability. He also makes an ego for everyone else he perceives, which is equally variable. Their interaction is a process*

*that alters both, because they were not made by or with the Unalterable.*

T51.2/56.2

*"Giving to get" is an inescapable law of the ego.*

T52.2/58.6

*The ego is quite literally a fearful thought. However ridiculous the idea of attacking God may be to the sane mind, never forget that the ego is not sane.*

T77.3/84.3

***Do not be afraid of the ego.** It depends on your mind, and as you made it by believing in it, so you can dispel it by withdrawing belief from it.*

T121.3/131.5

*Leave all illusions behind, and reach beyond all attempts of the ego to hold you back. I go before you because I am beyond the ego. Reach, therefore, for my hand because you want to transcend the ego. My strength will never be wanting, and if you choose to share it you will do so.*

T137.2/148.6

*Either God or the ego is insane.*

T179.1/193.1

Guess which!

*The ego can be completely forgotten at any time, because it is a totally incredible belief . . . The whole purpose of this Course is to teach you that the ego is unbelievable and will forever be unbelievable.*

T122.0 & .1/131.6 & .7

*The ego is trying to teach you how to gain the whole world and lose your own soul. The Holy Spirit teaches that you cannot lose your soul and there is no gain in the world, for of itself it profits nothing.*

T211.3/227.1

*The ego is certain that love is dangerous, and this is always its central teaching. It never puts it this way; on the contrary, everyone who believes that the ego is salvation seems to be intensely engaged in the search for love. Yet the ego, though encouraging the search for love very actively, makes one proviso; do not find it. Its dictates, then, can be summed up simply as: "Seek and do not find." . . . The Holy Spirit offers you another promise, and one that will lead to joy. For His promise is always, "Seek and you **will** find," and under His guidance you cannot be defeated.*

T207.4 & .7/223.1 & .4

*Every symptom the ego makes involves a contradiction in terms, because the mind is split between the ego and the Holy Spirit, so that whatever the ego makes is incomplete and contradictory.*

T43.2/48.7

*The ego is afraid of the spirit's joy, because once you have experienced it you will withdraw all protection from the ego, and become totally without investment in fear.*

T50.1/55.10

# Extension

Extension is the act of extending God's Love toward the world. This love comes from within you. God created you by extending Himself through you. You are an idea in the Mind of God.

> *To extend is a fundamental aspect of God which He gave to His Son. In the creation, God extended Himself to His creation and imbued them with the same loving will to create . . . The inappropriate use of extension or projection occurs when you believe that some emptiness or lack exists in you, and that you can fill it with your own ideas instead of truth.*
>
> T14.1/17.1

> *. . . without extension there can be no anger, but it is also true that without extension there can be no love.*
>
> T120.2/129.1

> *I gave only love to the Kingdom because I believed that was what I was. What you believe you are determines your gifts, and if God created you by extending Himself as you, you can only extend yourself as He did. Only joy increases forever, since joy and eternity are inseparable. God extends outward beyond limits and beyond time, and you who are co-creator with Him extend His Kingdom forever and beyond limit.*
>
> T104.5/113.5

> *As peace extends from deep inside yourself to embrace all the Sonship and give it rest, it will encounter many obstacles. Some of them you will try to impose. Others will seem to arise from elsewhere; from your brothers, and from various aspects of the world outside. Yet peace will gently cover them, extending past completely*

*unencumbered. The extension of the Holy Spirit's purpose from your relationship to others, to bring them gently in, is the way in which He will bring means and goal in line. The peace He lay, deep within you and your brother, will quietly extend to every aspect of your life, surrounding you and your brother with glowing happiness and the calm awareness of complete protection.*

T379.1/406.1

*To extend is a fundamental aspect of God which He gave to His Son. In the creation, God extended Himself to His creations and imbued them with the same loving Will to create.*

T14.1/17.1

*It still remains within you, however, to extend as God extended His Spirit to you. In reality this is your only choice, because your free will was given you for your joy in creating the perfect.*

T15.0/17.3

# Fear

Fear is the ego's tool. Fear weakens and separates you from your brothers. When you give yourself to fear, you lose your power. There are but two emotions according to the Course—Love and fear. Choose.

> *Perfect love casts out fear.*
> *If fear exists,*
> *Then there is not perfect love.*
> *But*
> *Only perfect love exists.*
> *If there is fear,*
> *It produces a state that does not exist.*
>
> T12.1/14.5

> *If you are trusting in your own strength, you have every reason to be apprehensive, anxious and fearful.*
>
> WB7.1/75.1

This is a great quote—reverse it. If you are feeling apprehensive, anxious or fearful, then you are holding the ego's hand. Your thinking is backwards. Hold the hands of Christ—let him lead you.

> *Nothing beyond yourself can make you fearful or loving, because nothing is beyond you.*
>
> T168.1/181.1

> *When you are afraid, be still and know that God is real, and you are His beloved Son in whom He is well pleased.*
>
> T49.3/55.0

You are held in God's Hands at all times. You are safe and loved. This is very comforting. You are in the world but you don't have to be *of* it. In times of stress, of loss, of stark, naked fear, you can be still and claim your Sonship, rather than your victimhood. You are not a victim of the world unless you choose to be.

> *You can never control the effects of fear yourself, because you made fear, and you believe in what you made.*

T11.4/14.4

You made fear and you have a lot invested in it. You are accustomed to it in all of its forms and the return to Love is fearful because you would have to change—change **is** the most frightening concept of all!

> *If you knew Who walks beside you on the way that you have chosen, fear would be impossible.*

T353.2/378.3

> *By applying the Holy Spirit's interpretation of the reactions of others more and more consistently, you will gain an increasing awareness that His criteria are equally applicable to you. For to recognize fear is not enough to escape from it, although the recognition is necessary to demonstrate the need for escape. The Holy Spirit must still translate the fear into truth. If you were left with the fear, once you had recognized it, you would have taken a step away from reality, not towards it. Yet we have repeatedly emphasized the need to recognize fear and face it without disguise as a crucial step in the undoing of the ego...He (Holy Spirit) has taught you that fear itself is an appeal for help. This is what recognizing fear really means. If you do not protect it, He will reinterpret it. That is the ultimate value in learning to perceive attack as a call for love. We have already learned that fear and attack are inevitably associated. If only attack produces fear, and if you see attack as the call for help that it is, the unreality of fear must dawn on you. For fear is a call for love, in unconscious recognition of what has been denied.*

T201.4/217.1

*Let us not be deceived today. We are the Sons of God. There is no fear in us, for we are each a part of Love Itself.*

WB402.3/412.3

*Fear is a symptom of your own deep sense of loss. If when you perceive it in others you learn to supply the loss, the basic cause of fear is removed. Thereby you teach yourself that fear does not exist in you. The means for removing it is in yourself, and you have demonstrated this by giving it. Fear and love are the only emotions of which you are capable. One is false, for it was made out of denial; and denial depends on the belief in what is denied for its own existence.*

T202.1/217.9

# Forgiveness

Forgiveness is most useful on this plane of existence, but is not a quality of God. God does not forgive because there is no need for it. He never condemned in the first place. You hold your brothers prisoner; they can never change in your eyes until your perception of them is forgiven (released). You hold a sword over your brother's head but it is actually over your own head. Forgiveness is recognizing that, despite appearances, nothing that needs forgiveness was done to forgive. Nothing your brother could do on the physical plane could affect your spiritual reality and your physical reality is but an illusion.

*You who want peace can find it only by complete forgiveness.*

T11.1/13.1

*Can you imagine how beautiful those you forgive will look to you? In no fantasy have you ever seen anything so lovely. Nothing you see here, sleeping or waking, comes near to such loveliness. And nothing will you value like unto this, nor hold so dear. Nothing that you remember that made your heart sing with joy has ever brought you even a little part of the happiness this sight will bring you. For you will see the Son of God. You will behold the beauty the Holy Spirit loves to look upon, and which He thanks the Father for. He was created to see this for you, until you learned to see it for yourself. And all His teaching leads to seeing it and giving thanks with Him.*

T328.3/352.1

*Ask not to be forgiven, for this has already been accomplished. Ask, rather, to learn how to forgive, and to restore what always was to your unforgiving mind.*

T260.1/279.3

*To forgive is merely to remember only the loving thoughts you gave in the past, and those that were given you . . . Forgiveness is a selective remembering, based not on your selection . . . Be willing to forgive the Son of God for what he did not do.*

T330.2/354.1

*The emptiness engendered by fear must be replaced by forgiveness. That is what the Bible means by "There is no death," and why I (Jesus) could demonstrate that death does not exist.*

T 9.2/16.4

Forgiveness *is for God and toward God but not of Him. It is impossible to think of anything He created that could need forgiveness. Forgiveness, then, is an illusion, but because of its purpose, which is the Holy Spirit's, it has one difference. Unlike all other illusions it leads away from error and not towards it.*

TM79.1/83.1

*Forgiveness paints a picture of a world where suffering is over, loss becomes impossible and anger makes no sense. Attack is gone, and madness has an end. What suffering is now conceivable? What loss can be sustained? The world becomes a place of joy, abundance, charity and endless giving. It is now so like to Heaven that it quickly is transformed into the light that it reflects. And so the journey which the Son of God began has ended in the light from which he came.*

WB408.1/418.1

# God

God cannot be defined. To attempt to define God is to limit Him to your beliefs about Him. God is often blamed, either directly or indirectly, for your sufferings and pain. Realize that God loves you; that you are His Son in whom He is well pleased. Love yourself with the Love of God.

You can make an idol out of just about anything, from cars, people, money, food, the Bible, or sex; you set these things up on pedestals and worship them. You lock up your cars, your houses, swearing to protect them with your lives, identifying yourself with them rather than God. What your Father wills for you has already been accomplished. He has answered all prayers before they have been made. You are but children, having nightmares and playing games until games became meaningless. Only the slightest of mists separates you from the truth. Be willing to have the mist dissolved for you. You don't even have to do anything. If you but knew the Home that awaits you, if you but got a glimpse, you could not wait.

> *The journey to God is merely the reawakening of the knowledge of where you are always, and what you are forever. It is a journey without distance to a goal that has never changed.*
>
> T139.3/150.9

> *God will come to you only as you will give Him to your brothers. Learn first of them and you will be ready to hear God.*
>
> T63.1/69.8

> *The recognition of God is the recognition of yourself. There is no separation of God and His creation.*
>
> T136.2/147.0

*God wants only his Son because His Son is His only treasure.*

T138/149

*God Himself is incomplete without me.*

T165.2/177.8

*Yet He* (God) *would not interfere with you, because He would not know His Son if he were not free.*

T177.4/191.10

*You cannot understand how much your Father loves you.*

T261.2/281.8

*God does not change His Mind about you, for He is not uncertain of Himself.*

T168.3/181.3

*There are no beginnings and no endings in God, Whose universe is Himself. Can you exclude yourself from the universe, or from God Who **is** the universe?*

T180.2/194.2

*To God all things are possible.*

T194.3/209.10

*Glory to God in the highest, and to you because He has so willed it. Ask and it shall be given you, because it has already been given. Ask for light and learn that you **are** light.*

T131.2/141.1

*Let us ask the Father in my name to keep you mindful of His Love for you and yours for Him. He has never failed to answer this request, because it asks only for what He has **already** willed. Those who call truly are always answered. Thou shalt have no other gods before Him because there are none.*

T55.4/61.6

*You can do nothing apart from Him, and you **do** do nothing apart from Him. Keep His way to remember yourself, and teach His way lest you forget yourself.*

*Give only honor to the Sons of the living God, and count yourself among them gladly.*

T119.0/128.5

*The Bible repeatedly states that you should praise God. This hardly means that you should tell Him how wonderful He is. He has no ego with which to accept such praise, and no perception with which to judge it. But unless you take your part in the creation, His joy is not complete because yours is incomplete . . . The constant going out of His Love is blocked when His channels are closed, and He is lonely when the minds He created do not communicate fully with Him.*

T64.3/70.6

*God is not a stranger to His Sons, and His Sons are not strangers to each other. Knowledge preceded both perception and time, and will ultimately replace them. That is the real meaning of "Alpha and Omega, the beginning and the end," and "Before Abraham was I am." Perception can and must be stabilized, but knowledge is stable. "Fear God and keep His commandments" becomes "Know God and accept His certainty."*

T36.4/41.6

God has only one Son—humankind.

*The statement "For God so loved the world that He gave His only begotten Son, that whosoever believeth in Him should not perish but have everlasting life" needs only one slight correction to be meaningful in this context; "He gave it **to** His only begotten Son."*

T28.3/33.5

*A Course in Miracles* – In a Nutshell

# God's Will

I had a difficult time early in my Course study in recognizing that my will is the same as God's. Now I know that my will _is_ God's Will. When I find myself in pain, then I know that I have lost my way and forgotten who I am.

*There is no difference between your will and God's.*

T150.1/161.5

The Holy Spirit is the comforter sent to you by God.

*There is no strain in doing God's Will as soon as you recognize that it is also your own.*

T26.1/30.6

*Fear of the Will of God is one of the strangest beliefs the human mind has ever made.*

T149.1/160.1

*Unless you hurt yourself you could never suffer in any way, for that is not God's Will for his Son. Pain is not of Him, for He knows no attack and His peace surrounds you silently. God is very quiet, for there is no conflict in Him. Conflict is the root of all evil, for being blind it does not see whom it attacks. Yet it always attacks the Son of God, and the Son of God is you.*

T184.2/198.1

*O my child, if you knew what God wills for you, your joy would be complete! And what He wills has happened, for it was always true. When the light comes and you have said, "God's Will is mine," you will see such beauty that you will know it is not of you. Out of your joy you will create beauty in His Name, for your joy could no more be contained than His.*

T184.4/199.3

*Even the relinquishment of your false decision-making prerogative, which the ego guards so jealously, is not accomplished by your wish. It was accomplished for you by the Will of God, Who has not left you comfortless.*

T125.3/135.7

*I said before that you are the Will of God. His Will is not an idle wish, and your identification with His Will is not optional, since it is what you are.*

T125.2./135.6

*Those who choose freedom will experience only its results. Their power is of God, and they will give it only to what God has given, to share with them. Nothing but this can touch them, for they see only this, sharing their power according to the Will of God.*

T403.3/432.4

# Grace

Grace is one of those concepts that I never thought much about because I didn't understand the concept. I think that the Course explains it very well in the quotes below.

*Spirit is in a state of grace forever.*

*Your reality is only spirit.*

*Therefore you are in a state of grace forever.*

T7.3/10.6

*Grace is not given to a body, but to a mind. And the mind that receives it looks instantly beyond the body, and sees the holy place where it was healed. There is the altar where the grace was given, in which it stands. Do you, then, offer grace and blessing to your brother, for you stand at the same altar where grace was laid for both of you. And be you healed by grace together, that you may heal through faith.*

T373.4/401.3

*Your grace is given me . . . I claim it now. If you but knew the meaning of His Love, hope and despair would be impossible. For hope would be forever satisfied; despair of any kind unthinkable. His grace His answer is to all despair, for in it lies remembrance of His Love. Would He not gladly give the means by which His Will is recognized? His grace is yours by your acknowledgment. And memory of Him awakens in the mind that asks the means of Him whereby its sleep is done.*

WB313.2/321.2

*And now in all your doings be you blessed.*

*God turns to you for help to save the world.*

*Teacher of God, His thanks He offers you,*

*And all the world stands silent in the grace*

*You bring from Him. You are the Son He loves,*

*And it is given you to be the means*

*Through which His Voice is heard around the world,*

*To close all things of time; to end the sight*

*Of all things visible; and to undo*

*All things that change. Through you is ushered in*

*A world unseen, unheard, yet truly there.*

*Holy are you, and in your light the world*

*Reflects your holiness, for you are not*

*Alone and friendless. I give thanks for you,*

*And join your efforts on behalf of God,*

*Knowing they are on my behalf as well,*

*And for all those who walk to God with me.*

TM69.1/72.1

# Grandeur vs. Grandiosity

Grandeur and grandiosity are terms the Course uses periodically. Grandeur is the God's Gift to us, while grandiosity is prideful posturing prodded by the ego. Weakness and littleness lurks behind the grandiose while the greatness of Spirit resides in the grandness of those who are expressing God's Love.

*Grandeur is of God, and only of Him. Therefore it is in you. Whenever you become aware of it, however dimly, you abandon the ego automatically, because in the presence of the grandeur of God the meaninglessness of the ego becomes perfectly apparent. When this occurs, even though it does not understand it, the ego believes that its "enemy" has struck, and attempts to offer gifts to induce you to return to its "protection." Self-inflation is the only offering it can make. The grandiosity of the ego is its alternative to the grandeur of God. Which will you choose?*

T165.3/177.1

*The ego is immobilized in the presence of God's grandeur, because His grandeur establishes your freedom. Even the faintest hint of your reality literally drives the ego from your mind, because you will give up all investment in it. Grandeur is totally without illusions, and because it is real it is compellingly convincing . . . The ego will make every effort to recover and mobilize its energies against your release. It will tell you that you are insane, and argue that grandeur cannot be a real part of you because of the littleness in which it believes. Yet your grandeur is not delusional because you did not make it. You made grandiosity and are afraid of it because it is a form of attack, but your grandeur is of God, Who created it out of His Love.*

*From your grandeur you can only bless, because your grandeur is your abundance. By blessing you hold it in your mind, protecting it from illusions and keeping yourself in the Mind of God. Remember always that you cannot be anywhere except in the Mind of God. When you forget this, you **will** despair and you **will** attack.*

*The ego depends solely on your willingness to tolerate it. If you are willing to look upon your grandeur you cannot despair, and therefore you cannot want the ego. Your grandeur is God's answer to the ego, because it is true. Littleness and grandeur cannot coexist, nor is it possible for them to alternate. Littleness and grandiosity can and must alternate, since both are untrue and are therefore on the same level.*

*Truth and littleness are denials of each other because grandeur is truth. Truth does not vacillate; it is always true. When grandeur slips away from you, you have replaced it with something you have made. Perhaps it is the belief in littleness; perhaps it is the belief in grandiosity. Yet it must be insane because it is not true. Your grandeur will never deceive you, but your illusions always will...It is easy to distinguish grandeur from grandiosity, because love is returned and pride is not. Pride will not produce miracles, and will therefore deprive you of the true witnesses to your reality . . . They attest to your grandeur, but they cannot attest to pride because pride is not shared.*

*Can your grandeur be arrogant when God Himself witnesses to it? And what can be real that has no witnesses? What good can come of it? And if no good can come of it the Holy Spirit cannot use it. What He cannot transform to the Will of God does not exist at all. Grandiosity is delusional, because it is used to replace your grandeur. Yet what God has created cannot be replaced. God is incomplete without you because His grandeur is total, and you cannot be missing from it.*

T166.2 – .7/178.4 – .9

# Gratitude

Gratitude and an attitude of thanksgiving are key concepts for making changes in life. They lighten your way and make easy your path. When you are grateful for all that you see and all that you experience without naming it as "good" or "bad," you grow spiritually.

> *Walk, then, in gratitude the way of love. For hatred is forgotten when we lay comparisons aside ...When your forgiveness is complete you will have total gratitude . . . For gratitude is but an aspect of the Love which is the Source of all creation. God gives thanks to you, His Son, for being what you are . . . For love can walk no road except the way of gratitude, and thus we go who walk the way to God.*
>
> WB363.2 & .4/373.8 & .10

> *Thanks be to you, the holy Son of God. For as you were created, you contain all things within your Self . . . All gratitude belongs to you, because of what you are.*
>
> WB368.2/378.8

> *In gratitude and thankfulness we come, with empty hands and open hearts and minds, asking but what You give.*
>
> WB442.4/452.2

> *I thank You, Father, for the many gifts that come to me today and every day from every Son of God. My brothers are unlimited in all their gifts to me. Now may I offer them my thankfulness, that gratitude to them may lead me on to my Creator and His memory.*
>
> WB448.2/458.2

*Love is the way I walk in gratitude. Gratitude is a lesson hard to learn for those who look upon the world amiss. The most that they can do is see themselves as better off than others. And they try to be content because another seems to suffer more than they. How pitiful and deprecating are such thoughts! For who has cause for thanks while others have less cause? And who could suffer less because he sees another suffer more? Your gratitude is due to Him alone Who made all cause of sorrow disappear throughout the world.*

WB362.1/372.1

*Gratitude is a lesson hard to learn for those who look upon the world amiss. The most that they can do is see themselves as better off than others. And they try to be content because another seems to suffer more than they. How pitiful and deprecating are such thoughts! For who has cause for thanks while others have less cause? And who could suffer less because he sees another suffer more? Your gratitude is due to Him alone Who made all cause of sorrow disappear throughout the world.*

T362.1/372.1

# Guilt

Guilt is a non-productive energy. It weakens you and strengthens low self-esteem. Guilt is a tool of the ego. He uses it to distract you from your greatness and sinless nature. You punish yourself for your mistakes; guilt is the weapon you use.

> *Guilt is more than merely not of God. It is the symbol of attack on God.*
>
> T77.2/84.0

> *Guilt is a sure sign that your thinking is unnatural.*
>
> T78.0/84.4

> *Guilt makes you blind, for while you see one spot of guilt within you, you will not see the light.*
>
> T244.2/262.7

> *Guilt must be given up, and not concealed. Nor can this be done without some pain, and a glimpse of the merciful nature of this step may for some time be followed by a deep retreat into fear.*
>
> Song of Prayer 5/S–1. III.4

Most of us carry a large burden of guilt below the surface, like an iceberg. Our brother becomes the scapegoat for that guilt. Forgive your brother and you forgive yourself and release some of your hidden burden of guilt that you have carried for so long.

> *The Son of God believes that he is lost in guilt, alone in a dark world where pain is pressing everywhere upon him from without. When he has looked within and seen the radiance there, he will remember how much his Father loves him. And it will seem incredible that he ever thought his Father loved him not.*
>
> T246.3/264.8

*As long as you believe that guilt is justified in any way, in anyone, whatever he may do, you will not look within, where you would always find Atonement. The end of guilt will never come as long as you believe there is a reason for it. For you must learn that guilt is always totally insane, and has no reason.*

T246.1/264.6

*Let me be to you the symbol of the end of guilt, and look upon your brother as you would look on me. Forgive me all the sins you think the Son of God committed. And in the light of your forgiveness he will remember who he is, and forget what never was. I ask for your forgiveness, for if you are guilty, so must I be. But if I surmounted guilt and overcame the world, you were with me. Would you see in me the symbol of guilt or of the end of guilt, remembering that what I signify to you, you see within yourself?*

T385.2/413.6

# Happiness

God's Will for you is perfect happiness. The Course tells us that the illusion of separation occurred when God's Son forgot how to laugh. The underlying message of the Course is for you to relax, just relax.

*The constancy of happiness has no exceptions; no change of any kind. It is unshakable as is the Love of God for His creation. Sure in its vision as its Creator is in what He knows, happiness looks on everything and sees it is the same. It sees not the ephemeral, for it desires everything be like itself, and sees it so. Nothing has power to confound its constancy, because its own desire cannot be shaken. It comes as surely unto those who see the final question is necessary to the rest, as peace must come to those who choose to heal and not to judge.*

T434.0/465.2

*Each idol that you worship when God calls will never answer in His place. There is no other answer you can substitute, and find the happiness His answer brings. Seek not outside yourself. For all your pain comes simply from a futile search for what you want, insisting where it must be found. What if it is not there? Do you prefer that you be right or happy? Be you glad that you are told where happiness abides, and seek no longer elsewhere. You will fail. But it is given you to know the truth, and not to seek for it outside yourself.*

T573.3/617.1

*The ego believes that to accomplish its goal is happiness. But it is given you to know that God's function is yours, and happiness cannot be found apart from Your joint Will. Recognize only that the ego's goal, which you have pursued so diligently, has merely brought you fear, and it becomes difficult to maintain that fear is happiness. Upheld by fear, this is what the ego would have you believe.*

T190.3/205.12

# Healing and Health

Healing is awakening and removing the blocks to true Vision. When one awakes to the Truth and remembers Who he is, then is he healed. Healing doesn't necessarily take place in the body; it always takes place in the mind.

*Healing is accomplished the instant the sufferer no longer sees any value in pain.*

TM16.2/17.1

*Health is the result of relinquishing all attempts to use the body lovelessly.*

T146.0/157.9

*Behold, my child, reality is here. It belongs to you and me and God, and is perfectly satisfying to all of us. Only this awareness heals, because it is the awareness of truth.*

T159.2/170.12

*To believe that a Son of God can be sick is to believe that part of God can suffer. Love cannot suffer, because it cannot attack.*

T171.3/185.3

*To heal is to make happy.*

T66.1/72.1

*Illness is some form of external searching. Health is inner peace.*

T15.2/18.5

*The rituals of the god of sickness are strange and very demanding. Joy is never permitted, for depression is the sign of allegiance to him. Depression means that* *you have forsworn God. Many are afraid of blasphemy, but they do not understand what it means. They do not realize that to deny God is to deny their own Identity, and in this sense the wages of sin **is** death. The sense is literal; denial of life perceives its opposite, as all forms of denial replace what is with what is not.*

T175.4/189.1

*You first forgive, then pray, and you are healed. Your prayer has risen up and called to God, Who hears and answers. You have understood that you forgive and pray but for yourself. And in this understanding you are healed. In prayer you have united with your Source, and understood that you have never left. This level cannot be attained until there is no hatred in your heart, and no desire to attack the Son of God.*

Song of Prayer 19/S–3.IV.4

# Heaven

Heaven is a state of mind You have the choice to experience Heaven right here on earth. Who knows what happens when you die. Why wait?

> *Heaven is here. There is nowhere else. Heaven is now. There is no other time.*
>
> TM58.2/61.6

> *"Heaven and earth shall pass away" means that they will not continue to exist as separate states. My word, which is the resurrection and the life, shall not pass away because life is eternal. You are the work of God, and His work is wholly lovable and wholly loving. This is how a man must think of himself in his heart, because this is what he is.*
>
> T6.3/9.2

> *You **are** the Kingdom of Heaven, but you have let the belief in darkness enter your mind and so you need a new light. The Holy Spirit is the radiance that you must let banish the idea of darkness.*
>
> T69.4/76.4

> *In Heaven, God's Son is not imprisoned in a body, nor is sacrificed in solitude to sin. And as he is in Heaven, so must he be eternally and everywhere. He is the same forever. Born again each instant, untouched by time, and far beyond the reach of any sacrifice of life or death.*
>
> T50.3/543.7

> *Seek ye first the Kingdom of Heaven, because that is where the laws of God operate truly, and they can operate only truly because they are the laws of truth.*

*But seek this only, because you can find nothing else. There is nothing else. God is All in all in a very literal sense. All being is in Him Who is all Being. You are therefore in Him since your being is His.*

T110.4/119.7

*It is hard to understand what "The Kingdom of Heaven is within you" really means. This is because it is not understandable to the ego, which interprets it as if something outside is inside and this does not mean anything. The word "within" is unnecessary. The Kingdom of Heaven is **you**. What else **but you** did the Creator create, and what else but you is His Kingdom? This is the whole message of the Atonement; a message which in its totality transcends the sum of its parts.*

T54.1/60.1

*When the temptation to attack rises to make your mind darkened and murderous, remember you **can** see the battle from above. Even in forms you do not recognize, the signs you know. There is a stab of pain, a twinge of guilt, and above all, a loss of peace. This you know well. When they occur leave not your place on high, but quickly choose a miracle instead of murder. And God Himself and all the lights of Heaven will gently lean to you, and hold you up.*

T462.5/497.5

*My true Identity is so secure, so lofty, sinless, glorious and great, wholly beneficent and free from guilt, that Heaven looks to It to give it light. It lights the world as well. It is the gift my Father gave to me; the one as well I give the world. There is no gift but this that can be either given or received. This is reality, and only this. This is illusion's end. It is the truth.*

WB393.3/403.3

# Hell

The concept of hell is often used to frighten little children into behaving themselves. It is used to blackmail people into following the rules that the church has set out for them. God is a Loving God, Who doesn't send people to hell. You **can** send yourself to hell if you so choose.

*The belief in hell is inescapable to those who identify with the ego. Their nightmares and their fears are all associated with it. The ego teaches that hell is in the future, for this is what all its teaching is directed to. Hell is its goal . . . The Holy Spirit teaches thus: There is no hell. Hell is only what the ego has made of the present. The belief in hell is what prevents you from understanding the present, because you are afraid of it.*

T280.4 & 281.3/301.4 & .7

*Let miracles replace all grievances. By this idea do I unite my will with the Holy Spirit's, and perceive them as one. By this idea do I accept my release from hell. By this idea do I express my willingness to have all my illusions be replaced with truth, according to God's plan for my salvation? I would make no exceptions and no substitutes. I want all of Heaven and only Heaven, as God wills me to have.*

WB152.3/154.3

*And so again we make the only choice that ever can be made; we choose between illusions and the truth, or pain and joy, or hell and Heaven. Let our gratitude unto our Teacher fill our hearts, as we are free to choose our joy instead of pain, our holiness in place of sin, the peace of God instead of conflict, and the light of Heaven for the darkness of the world.*

WB352.5/362.6

Heaven or hell is your choice to make. Keep your vision fixed firmly and resolutely upon Heaven, upon the Truth in you. Be vigilant. The Holy Instant is a little glimpse of Heaven as you open up to God and Christ more and more each day.

*Peace now belongs here, because a Thought of God has entered. What else but a Thought of God turns hell to Heaven merely by being what it is? The earth bows down before its gracious Presence, and it leans down in answer, to raise it up again. Now is the question different. It is no longer, "Can peace be possible in this world?" but instead, "Is it not impossible that peace be absent here?"*

TM28.4/30.1

*Earth can reflect Heaven or hell; God or the ego.*

T271.3./292.1

# Holiness

Holiness is wholeness, oneness with God. The holy have no need to attack because attack is prompted by fear, and the holy have nothing to fear. One thinks that if someone is seen as holy, he/she should be put up on a pedestal. This is a mistake because all are holy in Truth; underneath the layers of perceived "sin" is a perfect Child of God. There is no need for a pedestal.

*Before your brother's holiness the world is still, and peace descends on it in gentleness and blessing so complete that not one trace of conflict still remains to haunt you in the darkness of the night. He is your savior from the dreams of fear. He is the healing of your sense of sacrifice and fear that what you have will scatter with the wind and turn to dust. In him is your assurance God is here, and with you now. While he is what he is, you can be sure that God is knowable and will be known to you. For He could never leave His Own creation. And the sign that this is so lies in your brother, offered you that all your doubts about yourself may disappear before his holiness. See in him God's creation. For in him his Father waits for your acknowledgment that He created you as part of Him..*

T475.3/511.1

*Faith and belief and vision are the means by which the goal of holiness is reached. Through them the Holy Spirit leads you to the real world, and away from all illusions where your faith was laid. This is His direction; the only one He ever sees. And when you wander, He reminds you there is but one. His faith and His belief and vision are all for you. And when you have accepted them completely instead of yours, you will have need of them no longer. For faith and vision and belief are meaningful only before the state of certainty is reached. In Heaven they are unknown. Yet Heaven is reached through them.*

T421.4/452.4

# Holy Instant

The holy instant is a moment when a flash of intuition awakens one to a sense of unity with the universe. It can happen in many ways, but it does happen when you least expect it. It is a gift.

> The holy instant is a time in which you receive and give perfect communication. This means, however, that it is a time in which your mind is open, both to receive and give.
>
> T289.2/310.6

> In the holy instant, no one is special, for your personal needs intrude on no one to make your brothers seem different.
>
> T291.5/313.8

> The holy instant is the miracle's abiding place.
>
> T535.3/577.3

> The holy instant is a miniature of Heaven, sent you **from** Heaven.
>
> T335.4/360.11

> In the holy instant there are no bodies, and you experience only the attraction of God.
>
> T301.2/324.7

> In the holy instant, in which you see yourself as bright with freedom, you will remember God.
>
> T282.2/303.10

> For in the holy instant, free of the past, you see that love is in you, and you have no need to look without and snatch love guiltily from where you thought it was.

*All your relationships are blessed in the holy instant, because the blessing is not limited. In the holy instant, the Sonship gains as one and united in your blessing it becomes one to you.*

T292.1 & .2/314.9 & .10

*The holy instant does not come from your little willingness alone. It is always the result of your small willingness combined with the unlimited power of God's Will.*

T355.3/381.4

# Holy Relationship

The holy relationship is not something with which the world is familiar. It is not necessarily between a man and woman, because it is not based in duality—it is based on love. Those joining in a holy relationship are whole and complete, needing nothing from the outer world. Love flows forth from the relationship to bless the world.

*A holy relationship starts from a different premise. Each one has looked within and seen no lack. Accepting his completion, he would extend it by joining with another, whole as himself. He sees no differences between these selves, for differences are of the body.*

T435.2 & .3/467.2 & .3

*The holy relationship, a major step toward the perception of the real world, is learned. It is the old, unholy relationship, transformed and seen anew. The holy relationship is a phenomenal teaching accomplishment . . . Be comforted in this; the only difficult phase is the beginning. For here, the goal of the relationship is abruptly shifted to the exact opposite of what it was. This is the first result of offering the relationship to the Holy Spirit, to use for His purposes.*

T337.2/362.2

Most relationships begin as special relationships based on ego needs and body desires. When the two heal themselves to the point where they need nothing from the other and give their relationship over to the Holy Spirit, then they can share the holy relationship.

*Heaven is restored to all the Sonship through your relationship, for in it lies the Sonship, whole and beautiful, safe in your love. Heaven has entered quietly, for all illusions have been gently brought unto the truth in you, and love has shined upon you, blessing your relationship with truth. God and His whole creation have entered it together. How lovely and how holy is your relationship, with the truth shining upon it! Heaven beholds it, and rejoices that you have let it come to you.*

T349.3/374.11

*From your holy relationship truth proclaims the truth, and love looks on itself. Salvation flows from deep within the home you offered to my Father and to me. And we are there together, in the quiet communion in which the Father and the Son are joined. O come ye faithful to the holy union of the Father and the Son in you!*

T385.3/413.7

*The holy relationship reflects the true relationship the Son of God has with his Father in reality. The Holy Spirit rests within it in the certainty it will endure forever. Its firm foundation is eternally upheld by truth, and love shines on it with the gentle smile and tender blessing it offers to its own.*

T408.4/438.10

# Holy Spirit

The Holy Spirit is the Voice for God, created by God to offset the ego which came into being with the "separation." The Holy Spirit is the most useful tool you have at your disposal—give away your fear and pain to Him. He sees both levels—God's and man's—and can understand your problems and take them away. But He can take them away only if you **completely** release them.

> *If you cannot hear the Voice for God* (Holy Spirit), *it is because you do not choose to listen. That you* **do** *listen to the voice of your ego is demonstrated by your attitudes, your feelings and your behavior.*
>
> T57.1/62.1

> *The Holy Spirit is the Christ Mind which is aware of the knowledge that lies beyond perception.*
>
> T68.1/74.5

> *The Holy Spirit is the only part of the Holy Trinity that has a symbolic function. He is referred to as the Healer, the Comforter and the Guide. He is also described as something "separate," apart from the Father and from the Son. I myself said, "If I go I will send you another Comforter and He will abide with you."*
>
> T67.3/73.4

> *It is only because you think that you can run some little part, or deal with certain aspects of your life alone, that the guidance of the Holy Spirit is limited.*
>
> T277.2/298.8

> *The Holy Spirit is in you in a very literal sense. His is the Voice That calls you back to where you were before and will be again. It is possible even in this world to*

*hear only that Voice and no other...The Holy Spirit is the radiance that you must let banish the idea of darkness.*

T69.3 & .4/75.3 & .4

*The Holy Spirit's Voice is as loud as your willingness to listen.*

T145.4/157.8

*The Holy Spirit teaches one lesson, and applies it to all individuals in all situations. Being conflict free, He maximizes all efforts and all results. By teaching the power of the Kingdom of God Himself, He teaches you that all power is yours.*

T107.3/116.1

*The Holy Spirit is in your right mind, as He was in mine. The Bible says, "May the mind be in you that was also in Christ Jesus," and uses this as a blessing. It is the blessing of miracle-mindedness. It asks that you may think as I thought, joining with me in Christ thinking.*

T67.2/73.3

*Hear then, the one answer of the Holy Spirit to all the questions the ego raises: You are a child of God, a priceless part of His Kingdom, which He created as part of Him. Nothing else exists and only this is real. You have chosen a sleep in which you have had bad dreams, but the sleep is not real and God calls you to awake.*

T94.1/101.6

# Illusions

This world and all in it are but illusions, made from your imagination, to separate you from God. Look with your spiritual eyes to see the real meaning behind everything you see with your physical eyes.

*Illusions are but beliefs in what is not there.*

T312.2/335.4

*Your mind can be possessed by illusions, but spirit is eternally free.*

T9.9/11.2

*The only way to dispel illusions is to withdraw all investment from them, and they will have no life for you because you will have put them out of your mind.*

T118.3/127.4

*Faithlessness is wholly dedicated to illusions; faith wholly to truth. Partial dedication is impossible. Truth is the absence of illusion; illusion the absence of truth.*

T372.1/399.5

*If God knows His children as wholly sinless, it is blasphemous to perceive them as guilty. If God knows His children as wholly without pain, it is blasphemous to perceive suffering anywhere. If God knows His children to be wholly joyous, it is blasphemous to feel depressed. All of these illusions, and the many other forms that blasphemy may take, are refusals to accept creation as it is. If God created His Son perfect, that is how you must learn to see him to learn of his reality. And as part of the Sonship, that is how you must see yourself to learn of yours.*

T178.2/192.12

*The world you see is an illusion of a world. God did not create it, for what He creates must be eternal as Himself. Yet there is nothing in the world you see that will endure forever. Some things will last in time a little while longer than others. But the time will come when all things visible will have an end.*

TM81.1/85.1

*There is nothing you can hold against reality. All that must be forgiven are the illusions you have held against your brothers. Their reality has no past, and only illusions can be forgiven. God holds nothing against anyone, for He is incapable of illusions of any kind. Release your brothers from the slavery of their illusions by forgiving them for the illusions you perceive in them. Thus will you learn that you have been forgiven, for it is you who offered them illusions. In the holy instant this is done for you in time, to bring you the true condition of Heaven.*

T325.3/349.9

# Innocence

Innocence is a powerful concept. You are innocent because your Spirit is spotless, as God is Spotless, as He created you. No matter what your judgments of yourself are, no matter how guilty you feel, what your "sins" have been, you are still as God created you. The Truth will always remain True.

*"Except ye become as little children" means that unless you fully recognize your complete dependence on God, you cannot know the real power of the Son in his true relationship with the Father.*

T10.2/12.3

*The Bible tells you to become as little children. Little children recognize that they do not understand what they perceive, and so they ask what it means. Do not make the mistake of believing that you understand what you perceive, for its meaning is lost to you. Yet the Holy Spirit has saved its meaning for you, and if you will let Him interpret it, He will restore to you what you have thrown away. Yet while you think you know its meaning, you will see no need to ask it of Him.*

T196.1/211.2

*The lion and the lamb lying down together symbolize that strength and innocence are not in conflict, but naturally live in peace. "Blessed are the pure in heart for they shall see God" is another way of saying the same thing. A pure mind knows the truth and this is its strength.*

T33.2/37.5

# Invulnerability

You might tend to think of yourself as frail and liable to harm from all directions on the compass. If so, you are identifying yourself with your body. Of course, your body is vulnerable, but in your holiness your safety and invulnerability lie. The invulnerable know who they are—what their Truth is. They do not put out energy that invites attack. They have no buttons for people to push and no chips on their shoulders. The vulnerable identify with fear and fear invites attack like a magnet.

> *You are invulnerable because you are guiltless. You can hold on to the past only through guilt.*
>
> T222.3/238.8

> *The ego teaches you to attack yourself because you are guilty, and this must increase the guilt, for guilt is the result of attack. In the ego's teaching, then, there is no escape from guilt. For attack makes guilt real, and if it is real there is no way to overcome it. The Holy Spirit dispels it simply through the calm recognition that it has never been. As He looks upon the guiltless Son of God, He knows that this is true. And being true for you, you cannot attack yourself, for without guilt attack is impossible. You, then, are saved because God's Son is guiltless. And being wholly pure, you are invulnerable.*
>
> T223.2/239.11

> *Guiltlessness is invulnerability. Therefore, make your invulnerability manifest to everyone. Teach him that, whatever he may try to do to you, your perfect freedom from the belief that you can be harmed shows him that he is guiltless.*
>
> T256.3/275.7

# Joy

Joy and gladness are akin to love. Joy is found on the ecstatic face of those who celebrate life to its fullest. Joy is attractive; people want to be with those who are joy-filled. The joyous fill a room with light and love when they enter; they cannot hide their joy even if they wanted to.

*Joy is the inevitable result of gentleness. Gentleness means that fear is now impossible, and what could come to interfere with joy? The open hands of gentleness are always filled. The gentle have no pain. They cannot suffer. Why would they not be joyous? They are sure they are beloved and must be safe. Joy goes with gentleness as surely as grief attends attack. God's teachers trust in Him. And they are sure His Teacher goes before them, making sure no harm can come to them. They hold His gifts and follow in His way, because God's Voice directs them in all things. Joy is their song of thanks. And Christ looks down on them in thanks as well. His need of them is just as great as theirs of Him. How joyous it is to share the purpose of salvation!*

TM12.2/13.1

*Out of your joy you will create beauty in His Name, for your joy could no more be contained than His. The bleak little world will vanish into nothingness, and your heart will be so filled with joy that it will leap into Heaven, and into the Presence of God. I cannot tell you what this will be like, for your heart is not ready. Yet I can tell you, and remind you often, that what God wills for Himself He wills for you, and what He wills for you is yours.*

T184.3/199.3

# Judgment

There is a difference between evaluations and judgments. You evaluate the difference between blue and green, but judgment makes blue "bad" and green "good." Judgment either raises you above or puts you below another. Judgment of anything as "good" or "bad" prevents you from seeing the opportunity for healing in it. Judge not, for you have not all the facts of the situation—you have not walked a mile in your brother's shoes or looked at the situation from his point of view. The Course says that only God can judge. You are incapable of seeing your kindred as they truly are. You see a fault within yourself and project it outward and away from you and hide it in your brother. Then you blame him for what you cannot see in yourself. This becomes your opportunity, as you become more aware, to thank your brothers for showing you the dark places in yourself.

> You have no idea of the tremendous release and deep peace that comes from meeting yourself and your brothers totally without judgment.
>
> T42.2/47.3

> The ego cannot survive without judgment.
>
> T54.0/59.3

> When you feel tired, it is because you have judged yourself as capable of being tired. When you laugh at someone, it is because you have judged him as unworthy.
>
> T42.4/47.5

> Judgment always rests on the past; for past experience is the basis on which you judge.
>
> T290.1/312.1

*Do you prefer that you be right or be happy?*

T573.3/617.1

This quote can haunt you. It comes up over and over again in study groups, as students talk about their lives.

*Love makes no comparisons.*

WB362.4/372.4

*God's Final Judgment is as merciful as every step in His appointed plan to bless His Son, and call him to return to the eternal peace He shares with him.*

WB445.4/455.4

*..."By their fruits ye shall know them, and they shall know themselves." For it is certain that you judge yourself according to your teaching.*

T311.3/335.2

*If you perceive offense in a brother pluck the offense from your mind, or you are offended by Christ and are deceived in Him. Heal in Christ and be not offended by Him, for there is no offense in Him. If what you perceive offends you, you are offended in yourself and are condemning God's Son whom God condemneth not.*

T198.2/213.12

*I have said that judgment is the function of the Holy Spirit, and one He is perfectly equipped to fulfill. The ego as a judge gives anything but an impartial judgment.*

T144.3/156.4

*Judgment is symbolic because beyond perception there is no judgment. When the Bible says "Judge not that ye be not judged," it means that if you judge the reality of others you will be unable to avoid judging your own.*

*The choice to judge rather than to know is the cause of the loss of peace.*

T41.4 & .5/46.1 & .2

*The Last Judgment is generally thought of as a procedure undertaken by God. Actually it will be undertaken by my brothers with my help. It is a final healing rather than a meting out of punishment, however much you may think that punishment is deserved . . . The Last Judgment might be called a process of right evaluation. It simply means that everyone will finally come to understand what is worthy and what is not.*

T30.1/34.3

This illustrates the gentle and healing teaching that Christ does in the Course. You are, above all, your very own worst critic. You leap at every opportunity to hurt yourself and put yourself down. You are much kinder to your friends and even strangers, for the most part, than towards yourself. You think you deserve punishment and you are angry with yourself for having "sinned."

# Laws of Chaos

Chaos is a way of life for many people; they might be surprised to find that there are laws governing this state of being. The laws of chaos show how the ego justifies its existence. They show clearly how insane the world of illusion is and how God has been made the enemy from whom we must be "saved." Yet because we live in this world of illusion, we take them for laws of order. It is like looking in a warped mirror and seeing everything confused and opposite of what it truly is. The Course tells us it is important to look beyond them and to understand it is their purpose "to make meaningless and to attack the Truth." Since the quotes below are only a portion of the full text, you are encouraged to read the full version.

*The **first** chaotic law is that the truth is different for everyone. Like all these principles, this one maintains that each is separate and has a different set of thoughts that set him off from others. This principle evolves from the belief there is a hierarchy of illusions; some are more valuable and therefore true.*

*The **second** law of chaos, dear indeed to every worshipper of sin, is that each one must sin, and therefore deserves attack and death. This principle, closely related to the first, is the demand that errors call for punishment and not correction.*

*The arrogance on which the laws of chaos stand could not be more apparent than emerges here. Here is a principle that would define what the Creator of reality must be; what He must think and what He must believe; and how He must respond, believing it. It is not seen as even necessary that He be asked about the truth of what has been established for His belief. His Son can tell Him this, and He has but the choice whether to take his word for it or be mistaken. This* leads directly to the **third** preposterous belief that seems to make chaos eternal. For if God cannot be mistaken, He must accept His Son's belief in what he is, and hate him for it.

The ego values only what it takes. This leads to the **fourth** law of chaos, which, if the others are accepted, must be true. This seeming law is the belief you have what you have taken. By this, another's loss becomes your gain, and thus it fails to recognize that you can never take away save from yourself. Yet all the other laws must lead to this. For enemies do not give willingly to one another, nor would they seek to share the things they value. And what your enemies would keep from you must be worth having, because they keep it hidden from your sight.

. . . **final** principle of chaos . . . It holds there is a substitute for love. This is the magic that will cure all of your pain; the missing factor in your madness that makes it "sane." This is the reason why you must attack. Here is what makes your vengeance justified. Behold, unveiled, the ego's secret gift, torn from your brother's body, hidden there in malice and in hatred for the one to whom the gift belongs. He would deprive you of the secret ingredient that would give meaning to your life. The substitute for love, born of your enmity to your brother, must be salvation. It has no substitute, and there is only one. And all your relationships have but the purpose of seizing it and making it your own.

T455.1–456.5/489.1–.9


And yet, how can it be that laws like these can be believed? There is a strange device that makes it possible. Nor is it unfamiliar; we have seen how it appears to function many times before. In truth it does not function, yet in dreams, where only shadows play the major roles, it seems most powerful. No law of chaos could compel belief but for the emphasis on form and disregard of content. No one who thinks that one of these laws is true sees what it says. Some forms it takes seem to have meaning, and that is all.

T458.3/493.16

# Light

Light, as used in the Course, is understanding. The light banishes the darkness which is ignorance of God and Christ. Like a single candle in the darkest cave, the light shines forth to show the way through the doubts and fears that assail. The ego promotes confusion and cannot live in the light of understanding.

*Child of Light, you know not that the light is in you. Yet you will find it through its witnesses, for having given light to them they will return it. Each one you see in light brings your light closer to your awareness.*

T235.3/252.10

*Now is the time of salvation, for now is the release from time. Reach out to all your brothers, and touch them with the touch of Christ. In timeless union with them is your continuity, unbroken because it is wholly shared. God's guiltless Son is only light. There is no darkness in him anywhere, for he is whole. Call all your brothers to witness to his wholeness, as I am calling you to join with me. Each voice has a part in the song of redemption, the hymn of gladness and thanksgiving for the light to the Creator of light. The holy light that shines forth from God's Son is the witness that his light is of his Father.*

T235.1/252.8

*To you, then, light is crucial. While you remain in darkness, the miracle remains unseen. Thus you are convinced it is not there. This follows from the premises from which the darkness comes. Denial of light leads to failure to perceive it. Failure to perceive light is to perceive darkness. The light is useless to you then, even though it is there. You cannot use it because its presence is unknown to you. And the seeming reality of the darkness makes the idea of light meaningless.*

WB154.2/156.2

*I am the light of the world. How holy am I, who have been given the function of lighting up the world! Let me be still before my holiness. In its calm light let all my conflicts disappear. In its peace let me remember Who I am.*

*Let me not obscure the light of the world in me.*

*Let the light of the world shine through this appearance.*

*This shadow will vanish before the light.*

WB144.1/146.1

# Love

Christ was nothing but Love, and **A Course in Miracles** is a Course in Love. Love, like God, cannot be defined, but the Course has a great deal to say about it.

*The message of the crucifixion **is** perfectly clear: "Teach only love, for that is what you are."*

T87.2/94.13

*Love will enter immediately into any mind that truly wants it, but it must want it truly.*

T55.2/61.4

*Your task is not to seek for love, but merely to seek and find all the barriers within yourself that you have built against it.*

T315.1/338.6

*The holiest of all the spots on earth is where an ancient hatred has become a present love.*

T522.2/562.6

The quote above is a wonderful quote that emphasizes the importance of forgiveness and love!

*You are the work of God, and His work is wholly lovable and wholly loving. This is how a man must think of himself in his heart, because this is what he is.*

T7.0/9.2

*Be not afraid of love. For it alone can heal all sorrow, wipe away all tears, and gently waken from his dream of pain the Son whom God acknowledges as His. Be not afraid of this.*

WB445.4/455.4

*. . . exempt no one from your love, or you will be hiding a dark place in your mind where the Holy Spirit is not welcome. And thus you will exempt yourself from His healing power, for by not offering total love you will not be healed completely.*

T227.3/244.9

*Love is not special. If you single out part of the Sonship for your love, you are imposing guilt on all your relationships and making them unreal. You can love only as God loves. Seek not to love unlike Him, for there is no love apart from His.*

T247.2/265.11

# Magic

M agic is a belief in agents of healing that are outside you. That is not to say that healing is not done through medicines and surgery, but that the mind is so much more powerful than you could ever imagine. You can move mountains. You are infinite. You are omnipresent, omniscient, and omnipotent. There is nothing that you cannot do. However, until you really know this, if you need to go to a doctor, go to a doctor!

> *Healing only strengthens. Magic always tries to weaken.*
>
> T111.4/120.4

> *Magic is the mindless or the mis-creative use of mind.*
>
> T21.2/25.2

> *The body cannot create, and the belief that it can, a fundamental error, produces all physical symptoms. Physical illness represents a belief in magic.*
>
> T19.3/23.2

# Miracles

A miracle is a shift in perception—seeing a thing or a person in a new light. Some of the early lessons in the Workbook are concerned with being able to see the three-dimensional world from a different point of view. The miracle does not necessarily result in a change in the person or the thing or the event, but in the student's **reaction** to a person, a thing, or an event, which results in peace of mind. The 50 miracle principles at the beginning of *The Text* are supplemental reading to this section.

*Miracles are merely the translation of denial into truth.*

T203.1/218.1

*There is no order of difficulty in miracles. One is not "harder" or "bigger" than another.*

T1.1/3.1

This is an important idea. So many things appear too big and massive on this plane to change in any way. When you change your mind about them and your reactions to them, you will be pleasantly surprised at the miracles that result.

*You are part of Him Who is all power and glory, and are therefore as unlimited as He is.*

T131.0/141.7

**You** *are a miracle, capable of creating in the likeness of your Creator. Everything else* **is** *your own nightmare, and does not exist.*

T2.24/4.24

*A Miracle is never lost. It may touch many people you have not even met and produce undreamed of changes in situations of which you are not even aware.*

T4.45/6.45

Miracles go around the world as they are passed from person to person. A simple smile to a stranger can move him to change something drastic in his life.

*Miracles are natural. When they do not occur something has gone wrong.*

T1.6/3.6

*I raised the dead by knowing that life is an eternal attribute of everything that the living God created. Why do you believe it is harder for me to inspire the dis-spirited or to stabilize the unstable? I do not believe there is an order of difficulty in miracles; you do.*

T59.1/65.11

*Since miracles are but a shift in perception, how could one be more difficult than another? Only your disbelief closes your mind and makes them appear so.*

*The miracle thus has the unique property of abolishing time to the extent that it renders the interval of time it spans unnecessary. There is no relationship between the time a miracle takes and the time it covers. The miracle substitutes for learning that might have taken thousands of years. It does so by the underlying recognition of perfect equality of giver and receiver on which the miracle rests. The miracle shortens time by collapsing it, thus eliminating certain intervals within it. It does this, however, within the larger temporal sequence.*

T6.1/8.6

# Pain

Your pain and suffering are your choice—this is a tough lesson. Most often, the choice for pain is a subconscious one. Pain is real; there is no denying that it is real on the physical plane of existence, but not on the spiritual. This makes it part of the illusion. Do not be guilty; just choose once again!

> . . . nothing outside yourself can give you peace. It also means that nothing outside yourself can hurt you, or disturb your peace or upset you in any way.
>
> WB118.2/119.2

> It has been hopeless to attempt to find the hope of peace upon a battleground. It has been futile to demand escape from sin and pain of what was made to serve the function of retaining sin and pain. For pain and sin are one illusion, as are hate and fear, attack and guilt but one. Where they are causeless their effects are gone, and love must come wherever they are not. Why are you not rejoicing? You are free of pain and sickness, misery and loss, and all effects of hatred and attack. No more is pain your friend and guilt your god, and you should welcome the effects of love.
>
> T565.3/609.3

I love the question "Why are you not rejoicing?" Live in the 'now' moment—there can be no pain there.

> Sin shifts from pain to pleasure, and again to pain. For either witness is the same, and carries but one message: "You are here, within this body, and you can be hurt. You can have pleasure, too, but only at the cost of pain." These witnesses are joined by many more. Each one seems different because it has a different name, and so it seems to answer to a different sound. Except for this, the witnesses of sin are all

*alike. Call pleasure pain, and it will hurt. Call pain a pleasure, and the pain behind the pleasure will be felt no more. Sin's witnesses but shift from name to name as one steps forward and another back. Yet which is foremost makes no difference. Sin's witnesses hear but the call of death.*

T537.1/ 579.2

*The shadowy figures from the past are precisely what you must escape. They are not real, and have no hold over you unless you bring them with you. They carry the spots of pain in your mind, directing you to attack in the present in retaliation for a past that is no more. And this decision is one of future pain. Unless you learn that past pain is an illusion, you are choosing a future of illusions and losing the many opportunities you could find for release in the present. The ego would preserve your nightmares, and prevent you from awakening and understanding they are past.*

T229.3/246.6

# Peace

Peace can be seen anywhere you look when you drop judgment and ego thoughts. Peace is all around and within you right now, in this chaotic world. Wake up! All you need do is nothing, and it is yours! Peace is your natural heritage. It comes with your creation. You cannot lose your peace. You can, however, give it away, but In reality, it is forever with you.

> *The peace of God is everything I want. The peace of God is my one goal; the aim of all my living here, the end I seek, My purpose and my function and my life while I abide where I am not at home.*
>
> WB380.1/390.1

> *You can do anything I ask. I have asked you to perform miracles, and have made it clear that miracles are natural, corrective, healing and universal. There is nothing they cannot do, but they cannot be performed in the spirit of doubt or fear. When you are afraid of anything, you are acknowledging its power to hurt you. Remember that where your heart is, there is your treasure also. You believe in what you value. If you are afraid, you are valuing wrongly. Your understanding will then inevitably value wrongly, and by endowing all thoughts with equal power will inevitably destroy peace. That is why the Bible speaks of "the peace of God which passeth understanding." This peace is totally incapable of being shaken by errors of any kind. It denies the ability of anything not of God to affect you.*
>
> T15.3/19.1

There is nothing wrong with the treasures of this world. The Course continually emphasizes the truth about you, the truth about your life, the truth about your existence here. And that truth is buried by your judgments of yourself and the world. You are trained from birth to value certain things, to expect certain results from certain causes. But the things of this world are transient at best, including your body. God is the Cause. You are His Results. Put faith and trust in the only permanence there is, God. When this happens, peace is the inevitable result. Fear, the Course tells you, is the result when you put your faith in yourself.

*Peace be unto you who rest in God, and in whom the whole Sonship rests.*

T187.4/202.8

*Only at the altar of God will you find peace. And this altar is in you because God put it there. His Voice still calls you to return, and He will be heard when you place no other gods before Him.*

T173.2/187.4

*You who want peace can find it only by complete forgiveness.*

T11.2/13.1

*There is a place in you where this whole world has been forgotten; where no memory of sin and of illusion lingers still. There is a place in you which time has left and echoes of eternity are heard. There is a resting place so still no sound except a hymn to Heaven rises up to gladden God the Father and the Son. Where both abide are They remembered, Both. And where They are is Heaven and is peace.*

T570.2/614.1

*When I said, "My peace I give unto you," I meant it. Peace comes from God through me to you.*

T172.2/185.6

*The peace of God passeth your understanding only in the past. Yet here it is, and you can understand it now. God loves His Son forever, and His Son returns his Father's Love forever.*

T238.1/255.8

*You will not find peace until you have removed the nails from the hands of God's Son, and taken the last thorn from his forehead.*

T193.4/208.7

The "nails" and "thorns" are the judgments you have placed upon your brother.

*Think not you understand anything until you pass the test of perfect peace, for peace and understanding go together and never can be found alone.*

*Whenever you think you know, peace will depart from you, because you will have abandoned the Teacher of peace.*

T278.3 & .4/299.2 & .3

# Perception

The Course emphasizes repeatedly that your physical eyes do not see the Truth of yourself, the world, your brother, or events around you. Your eyes are blinded by your perceptions and past thinking. You see what you wish to see, and are led by your erroneous thinking into the circles and cycles of an endless maze—until you realize that your true perception comes when you close your physical eyes and see with your spiritual perception.

> *What you perceive in others, you are strengthening in yourself.*
>
> T73.4/80.9

> *He (God) has no ego with which to accept . . . praise and no perception with which to judge it.*
>
> T64.3/70.6

> *Beware of the temptation to perceive yourself unfairly treated.*
>
> T523.3/563.4

The world is an illusion—a fairy tale—it is insane. Trying to make sense of it and asking it to be fair to you simply intensifies the insanity because it drags you further into it.

> *The way to correct distortions* (wrong perception) *is to withdraw your faith in them and invest it only in what is true.*
>
> T35.2/39.6

> *Perception is consistent. What you see reflects your thinking. And your thinking but reflects your choice of what you want to see. Your values are determiners of this, for what you value you must want to see, believing what you see is really there. No one can see a*

*world his mind has not accorded value. And no one can fail to look upon what he believes he wants.*

WB231.1/237.1

*You do not know the meaning of anything you perceive. Not one thought you hold is wholly true . . . Instruction in perception is your great need, for you understand nothing.*

T196.2/211.3

*Your brother is the mirror in which you see the image of yourself as long as perception lasts. And perception will last until the Sonship knows itself as whole.*

T118.2/127.3

*You respond to what you perceive, and as you perceive so shall you behave. The Golden Rule asks you to do unto others as you would have them do unto you. This means that the perception of both must be accurate. The Golden Rule is the rule for appropriate behavior. You cannot behave appropriately unless you perceive correctly. Since you and your neighbor are equal members of one family, as you perceive both so you will do to both. You should look out from the perception of your own holiness to the holiness of others.*

T7.4/10.6

*It is impossible not to believe what you see, but it is equally impossible to see what you do not believe. Perceptions are built up on the basis of experience, and experience leads to beliefs. It is not until beliefs are fixed that perceptions stabilize. In effect, then, what you believe you **do** see. That is what I meant when I said, "Blessed are ye who have not seen and still believe," for those who believe in the resurrection will see it.*

T192.1/207.1

*Projection makes perception. The world you see is what you gave it, nothing more than that. It is the witness to your state of mind, the outside picture of an inward condition. As a man thinketh, so does he perceive.*

*Therefore, seek not to change the world, but choose to change your mind about the world.*

T415.1/445.1

The last sentence in this quote has been very meaningful to me. It is not the world that is the problem, but your reaction to the world. Your thoughts make your world. If you experience attack thoughts, then attack is what you experience. If you think loving thoughts, then love is what you see.

# Persecution

Persecution can only occur in the worldly illusion. One who is persecuted is experiencing fears which includes the loss of safety, aloneness, and death. You are indeed safe in the Hands of God, therefore you could never be alone, and what God created could never die.

> *"As you teach so shall you learn." If you react as if you are persecuted, you are teaching persecution. This **is** not a lesson a Son of God should want to teach if he **is** to realize his own salvation.*

T85.4/93.6

You are in charge of only one thing—yourself—and how you react to situations and events.

> *The message the crucifixion was intended to teach was that it is not necessary to perceive any form of assault in persecution, because you cannot be persecuted. If you respond with anger, you must be equating yourself with the destructible, and are therefore regarding yourself insanely.*

T85.2/92.4

# Power

The ego would have you look to your body and your brain for power. Power is of God. His Power has been given you so that you can create through your mind. Your creations are your loving thoughts.

*Few appreciate the real power of the mind, and no one remains fully aware of it all the time. However, if you hope to spare yourself from fear there are some things you must realize, and realize fully. The mind is very powerful, and never loses its creative force. It never sleeps. Every instant it is creating. It is hard to recognize that thought and belief combine into a power surge that can literally move mountains. It appears at first glance that to believe such power about yourself is arrogant, but that is not the real reason you do not believe it. You prefer to believe that your thoughts cannot exert real influence because you are actually afraid of them. This may allay awareness of the guilt, but at the cost of perceiving the mind as impotent. If you believe that what you think is ineffectual you may cease to be afraid of it, but you are hardly likely to respect it. There are no idle thoughts. All thinking produces form at some level.*

T27.1/31.9

*The power set in you in whom the Holy Spirit's goal has been established is so far beyond your little conception of the infinite that you have no idea how great the strength that goes with you. And you can use this in perfect safety. Yet for all its might, so great it reaches past the stars and to the universe that lies beyond them, your little faithlessness can make it useless, if you would use the faithlessness instead.*

T344.1/369.7

*Would you not want to make a holy instant of every situation? For such is the gift of faith, freely given wherever faithlessness is laid aside, unused. And then the power of the Holy Spirit's purpose is free to use instead. This power instantly transforms all situations into one sure and continuous means for establishing His purpose, and demonstrating its reality. What has been demonstrated has called for faith, and has been given it. Now it becomes a fact, from which faith can no longer be withheld. The strain of refusing faith to truth is enormous, and far greater than you realize. But to answer truth with faith entails no strain at all.*

T345.3/370.3

# Prayer

Prayer in the Course becomes merely communication between you and your Father. The Voice for God, the Holy Spirit, facilitates the process and it is most effective when you just become still and listen. You may not hear a voice, but you may get an idea, or a nudge, or an inspiration—whatever form the answer takes is perfect.

*I am here only to be truly helpful.*

*I am here to represent Him who sent me.*

*I do not have to worry about what to say or what to do, because He*

*Who sent me will direct me.*

*I am content to be wherever He wishes, knowing He goes there with me.*

*I will be healed as I let Him teach me to heal.*

T24.3/28.8

This is a wonderful prayer. When you are open to letting Him speak through and use you, you need not worry about the outcome—it is done in God's perfect time and perfect order.

*Forgive us our illusions, Father, and help us to accept our true relationship with You, in which there are no illusions, and where none can ever enter. Our holiness is Yours. What can there be in us that needs for-giveness when Yours is perfect? The sleep of for-getfulness is only the unwillingness to remember Your forgiveness and Your Love. Let us not wander into temptation, for the temptation of the Son of God is not Your Will. And let us receive only what You have given, and accept but this into the minds which You created and which You love. Amen.*

The prior quote is a rewording of the Lord's Prayer.

> *The Bible emphasizes that all prayer is answered, and this is indeed true. The very fact that the Holy Spirit has been asked for anything will ensure a response. Yet it is equally certain that no response given by Him will ever be one that would increase fear . . . There are many answers you have already received but have not yet heard. I assure you that they are waiting for you.*
>
> T152.4/164.3

The answer to every prayer is in the pray-er, the one who is praying.

# Projection

Projection is the act of the interpreting the world out of one's own ideas of what the world should be. You often see through tainted glasses. What you see with your physical eyes deceives you.

> *The difference between the ego's projection and the Holy Spirit's extension is very simple. The ego projects to exclude, and therefore to deceive. The Holy Spirit extends by recognizing Himself in every mind, and thus perceives them as one.*
>
> T91.1/98.12

> *The ultimate purpose of projection is always to get rid of guilt.*
>
> T223.3/23.1

You project your guilt onto a wife, for example, trying to get rid of it, hiding it in her. Then you resent her without realizing it is **your** guilt that you resent.

> *Ideas leave not their source, and their effects but seem to be apart from them. Ideas are of the mind. What is projected out, and seems to be external to the mind, is not outside at all, but an effect of what is in, and has not left its source.*
>
> T515.2/554.4

# Reality

Reality is what God created. What you see with your physical eyes is subject to destruction in many forms. Love, Peace, Joy, and Abundance—characteristics of God—are what the Course calls real. They are changeless qualities.

> *What can be fearful but fantasy, and who turns to fantasy unless he despairs of finding satisfaction in reality? Yet it is certain that you will never find satisfaction in fantasy, so that your only hope is to change your mind about reality. Only if the decision that reality is fearful is wrong can God be right. And I assure you that God is right. Be glad, then, that you have been wrong, but this was only because you did not know who you were. Had you known, you could no more have been wrong than God can.*
>
> T158.5/170.10

> *Reality is never frightening. It is impossible that it could upset me. Reality brings only perfect peace. When I am upset, it is always because I have replaced reality with illusions I made up. The illusions are upsetting because I have given them reality, and thus regard reality as an illusion. Nothing in God's creation is affected in any way by this confusion of mine. I am always upset by nothing.*
>
> WB83.1/84.1

The previous quote is an affirmation for you to use.

> *Anger but screeches, "Guilt is real!" Reality is blotted out as this insane belief is taken as replacement for God's Word. The body's eyes now "see"; its ears alone can "hear." Its little space and tiny breath become the*

*measure of reality. And truth becomes diminutive and meaningless. Correction has one answer to all this, and to the world that rests on this.*

TM45.3/47.3

# Redemption

This is another of the Biblical terms which the Course uses and which turn away so many potential students who are revolting against fundamental religion and the old Biblical teachings. According to those teachings, when you are redeemed, you are excused from your "sins" and hell and made eligible for Heaven. According to the Course, you are eligible for Heaven regardless of your "sins" which it calls mistakes. When one makes a mistake, all he need to do is to make another choice and another perception.

> Be you content with healing, for Christ's gift you can bestow, and your Father's gift you cannot lose. Offer Christ's gift to everyone and everywhere, for miracles, offered the Son of God through the Holy Spirit, attune you to reality. The Holy Spirit knows your part in the redemption, and who are seeking you and where to find them. Knowledge is far beyond your individual concern. You who are part of it and all of it need only realize that it is of the Father, not of you. Your role in the redemption leads you to it by re-establishing its oneness in your mind.
>
> T242.1/259.7

> I was a stranger and you took me in, not knowing who I was. Yet for your gift of lilies you will know. In your forgiveness of this stranger, alien to you and yet your ancient Friend, lies his release and your redemption with him. The time of Easter is a time of joy, and not of mourning. Look on your risen Friend, and celebrate his holiness along with me. For Easter is the time of your salvation, along with mine.
>
> T396.4/425.4

# Resurrection

Christ tells us in the Course to focus on the resurrection, not the persecution or the crucifixion.

> *Yet every instant can you be reborn, and given life again.*
>
> T505.3/543.7

> *Your resurrection is your reawakening. I (Christ) am the model for rebirth, but rebirth itself is merely the dawning on your mind of what is already in it. God placed it there Himself, and so it is true forever.*
>
> T86.1/93.7

> *The resurrection is the complete triumph of Christ over the ego, not by attack but by transcendence. For Christ does rise above the ego and all its works, and ascends to the Father and His Kingdom.*
>
> T192.1/207.1

> *Believe in the resurrection because it has been accomplished, and it has been accomplished in you. For we ascend unto the Father together, as it was in the beginning, is now and ever shall be, for such is the nature of God's Son as His Father created him.*
>
> T193.1/208.4

# Revelation

Revelation is direct communication from Spirit—insight, spiritual understanding, and an overwhelming sense of Love is imparted during revelation.

*Revelation unites you directly with God.*

T4.12/7.1

*Revelation is literally unspeakable because it is an experience of unspeakable love.*

T5.2/7.2

*Revelation induces complete but temporary suspension of doubt and fear. It reflects the original form of communication between God and His creations . . . Revelation unites you directly with God.*

T4.12/7.1

*Miracles are a way of earning release from fear. Revelation induces a state in which fear has already been abolished. Miracles are thus a means and revelation is an end.*

T3.28/5.28

*God has kept your Kingdom for you, but He cannot share His joy with you until you know it with your whole mind. Revelation is not enough, because it is only communication from God. God does not need revelation returned to Him, which would clearly be impossible, but He does want it brought to others. This cannot be done with the actual revelation; its content cannot be expressed, because it is intensely personal to the mind that receives it.*

T64.4/71.7

# Sacrifice

God requests no sacrifices of you except to give up your attack thoughts.

*All sacrifice entails the loss of your ability to see relationships among events. And looked at separately they have no meaning. For there is no light by which they can be seen and understood. They have no purpose. And what they are for cannot be seen.*

T597.1/642.6

*In His* (Christ's) *Presence the whole Idea of sacrifice loses all meaning. For He is Host to God.*

T304.2/327.2

You are also Host to God!

*Sacrifice is so essential to your thought system that salvation apart from sacrifice means nothing to you. Your confusion of sacrifice and love is so profound that you cannot conceive of love without sacrifice. And it is this that you must look upon; sacrifice is attack, not love.*

T302.4/325.5

# Safety

Safety comes from within, rather than without.

> *This is the question that* must *be asked: "Where can I go for protection?" "Seek and ye shall find" does not mean that you should seek blindly and desperately for something you would not recognize. Meaningful seeking is consciously undertaken, consciously organized and consciously directed.*
>
> T60.3/66.5

Conscious organization and direction imply consciousness of spiritual unity with your Creator. To have a direction, a goal is implied. The goals that the Course recommends are peace, love, joy, and happiness. When your path is set firmly toward those goals, the whole power of the universe sails with you.

> *Light does not attack darkness, but it does shine it away. If my light goes with you everywhere, you shine it away with me. The light becomes ours, and you cannot abide in darkness any more than darkness can abide wherever you go.*
>
> T134.0/144.2

# Salvation

The good news is that there is nothing from which to be saved! Salvation is releasing ego thoughts and achieving inner peace in spite of all of the chaos and turmoil around you. Salvation is uniting with Christ as your elder brother and following his footsteps.

> *Salvation is nothing more than "right-minded-ness,"* . . .
> *which must be achieved before One-minded-ness is restored.*
>
> T53.3/59.10

> *The secret of salvation is but this: That you are doing this unto yourself.*
>
> T545.4/587.11

Crucify yourself no more, you Holy Child of God! You are your own salvation.

> *Salvation is accomplished. Freedom from conflict has been given you. Accept that fact, and you are ready to take your rightful place in God's plan for salvation.*
>
> T141.1/143.1

# Second Coming

The Second Coming of Christ is highly anticipated by many, but it is not the end of the world. You don't have to wait any more—he is with you right now.

*The Second Coming is merely the return of sense.*

T158.4/170.9

*The First Coming of Christ is merely another name for the creation, for Christ is the Son of God. The Second Coming of Christ means nothing more than the end of the ego's rule and the healing of the mind.*

T58.4/64.10

# Separation

The idea of separation is the ego's major tool to keep you unaware of your true nature as a Child of God. You are so much greater than the world sees you or you see yourself. Accept your divinity and rise above the drama and trauma of the world.

*The journey to God is merely the awakening of the knowledge of where you are always, and what you are forever. It is a journey without distance to a goal that has never changed.*

T139.3/150.9

*The recognition of God is the recognition of yourself. There is no separation of God and His creation.*

T136.2/147.0

*A sense of separation from God is the only lack you really need correct.*

T11.2/14.2

You could never be truly separated from God!

*God Himself is incomplete without me.*

T165.1/177.8

# Sin

"Sin" is an acronym for **S**elf **I**nflicted **N**onsense. It is an old archer's term for "missing the mark." None of you are "sinners." You have made mistakes, simply acted against your own best interests and the interests of others out of ignorance of the true nature of the universe. When you miss the mark, simply take out another arrow and aim again.

> *Darkness is lack of light as sin is lack of love.*
>
> T9.1/11.3

> *Son of God, you have not sinned, but you have been much mistaken.*
>
> T176.5/190.6

> *No one is punished for sins, and the Sons of God are not sinners.*
>
> T88.0/95.16

> *The Son of God can be mistaken; he can deceive himself; he can even turn the power of his mind against himself. But he **cannot** sin. There is nothing he can do that would really change his reality in any way, nor make him really guilty. That is what sin would do, for such is its purpose. Yet for all the wild insanity inherent in the whole idea of sin, it is impossible. For the wages of sin is death, and how can the immortal die?*
>
> T375.2/402.3

The concept of sin was developed to keep the congregant from wandering away from the church. The "sinner" is made to feel guilty and apply to the church for forgiveness.

> *To witness sin and yet forgive it is a paradox that reason cannot see. For it maintains what has been*

*done to you deserves no pardon. And by giving it, you grant your brother mercy but retain the proof he is not really innocent. The sick remain accusers. They cannot forgive their brothers and themselves as well. For no one in whom true forgiveness rests can suffer. He holds not the proof of sin before his brother's eyes. And thus he must have overlooked it and removed it from his own.*

T528/569.3

This reminds me of the Biblical line about removing the mote from someone else's eye, while ignoring the tree that is in your own.

*The statement "Vengeance is Mine, sayeth the Lord" is a misperception by which one assigns his own "evil" past to God. The "evil" past has nothing to do with God. He did not create it and He does not maintain it. God does not believe in retribution. His Mind does not create that way. He does not hold your "evil" deeds against you . . . This kind of error is responsible for a host of related errors, including the belief that God rejected Adam and forced him out of the Garden of Eden.*

T32.3/36.3

God does not see your "evil" side. He sees only His Son, in whom He is well pleased, with whom He endowed His own Peace, Abundance, Love, and Joy.

*"I will visit the sins of the fathers unto the third and fourth generation," as interpreted by the ego, is particularly vicious. It becomes merely an attempt to guarantee the ego's own survival. To the Holy Spirit, the statement means that in later generations He can still reinterpret what former generations had misunderstood, and thus release the thoughts from the ability to produce fear.*

T80.6/87.8

This has implications for you that the miracle, or the shift in perception, can have healing effects within your life, for as you see your past differently, you remove the pain and guilt associated with those past events, thus healing retroactively.

*Yet if the Holy Spirit can commute each sentence that you laid upon yourself into a blessing, then it cannot be a sin. Sin is the only thing in all the world that cannot change. It is immutable. And on its changelessness the world depends. The magic of the world can seem to hide the pain of sin from sinners, and deceive with glitter and with guile. Yet each one knows the cost of sin is death. And so it is. For sin is a request for death, a wish to make this world's foundation sure as love, dependable as Heaven, and as strong as God Himself.*

T494.1/531.1

I believe in the original blessing, not the original sin!

# Specialness

Beware of a sense of specialness. In **A Course in Miracles**, all of humankind are part of the Sonship, all essentially one Child of God. Specialness is the distinguishing of one from the other based upon physical, mental, or political differences. The ego delights in division! The ego would have us all be "special" and apart. God sees us all as His Perfect and Holy Children, in whom He is well pleased. He does not see the special characteristics that we have made in our lives, because He did not create them.

> Specialness is the great dictator of the wrong decisions. Here is the grand illusion of what you are and what your brother is. And here is what must make the body dear and worth preserving. Specialness must be defended. Illusions can attack it, and they do. For what your brother must become to keep your specialness **is** an illusion. He who is "worse" than you must be attacked, so that your specialness can live on his defeat. For specialness is triumph, and its victory is his defeat and shame. How can he live, with all your sins upon him? And who must be his conqueror but you?
>
> T465.3/500.5

Certainly there are physical differences between us—color, race, possessions, position in life, physical perfections or imperfections, but the idea of this message is to encourage you not to dwell on and focus upon the differences, but upon the samenesses. Spirit is alive in all—the President of the United States is no more special than the lowest criminal in prison. They simply have chosen different experiences in the illusion. The ego in you will tend to get very upset when you think of your special situation, whatever it may be, but Love sees no specialness.

> Pursuit of specialness is always at the cost of peace. Who can attack his savior and cut him down, yet

*recognize his strong support? Who can detract from his omnipotence, yet share his power? And who can use him as the gauge of littleness, and be released from limits? You have a function in salvation. Its pursuit will bring you joy. But the pursuit of specialness must bring you pain. Here is a goal that would defeat salvation, and thus run counter to the Will of God. To value specialness is to esteem an alien will to which illusions of yourself are dearer than the truth.*

T467.1/502.2

Any time you judge yourself to be above or below someone else, think again! Join with him/her in love and friendship. Look with different eyes on people far and near. Watch the news and see those on the TV with different eyes and hear them with different ears. Any time you judge you are giving a thorn (pain); when you unify you are giving a lily (love) to your brother.

# Special Relationship

The "special relationship" is based on ego and each person in this kind of relationship is seeking to find his salvation in the other person. Each person is looking for a missing part of himself in the other, and is inevitably disappointed. Pain, therefore, is a necessary result of forming special relationships.

> *For an unholy relationship is based on differences, where each one thinks the other has what he has not. They come together, each to complete himself and rob the other. They stay until there is nothing left to steal, and then move on.*
>
> T435.2 & .3/467.2 & .3

> *In looking at the special relationship, it is necessary first to realize that it involves a great amount of pain. Anxiety, despair, guilt and attack all enter into it, broken into by periods in which they seem to be gone . . . Whatever form they take, they are always an attack on the self to make the other guilty.*

> *The special love relationship is the ego's most boasted gift, and one which has the most appeal to those unwilling to relinquish guilt.*
>
> T317.1 & .3/341.1 & .3

# Suffering

Poor, poor, pitiful me! Mia Culpa! Your suffering is but a call for you to awaken from the nightmares of this world. It is very easy to go unconscious with busy-ness with the activities here, but take time to be still and be *in* the world but not *of* it.

> *The only message of the crucifixion is that you can overcome the cross. Until then you are free to crucify yourself as often as you choose.*
>
> T47.3/52.3

> *How can you who are so holy suffer? All your past except its beauty is gone, and nothing is left but a blessing. I have saved all your kindnesses and every loving thought you ever had. I have purified them of the errors that hid their light, and kept them for you in their own perfect radiance.*
>
> T7.3/8.8

> *. . . nothing outside yourself can save you; nothing outside yourself can give you peace . . . nothing outside yourself can hurt you, or disturb your peace or upset you in any way.*
>
> WB118.2/119.2

> *Illusion recognized must disappear. Accept not suffering, and you remove the thought of suffering. Your blessing lies on everyone who suffers, when you choose to see all suffering as what it is. The thought of sacrifice gives rise to all the forms that suffering appears to take. And sacrifice is an idea so mad that sanity dismisses it at once.*
>
> WB346.1/355.7

*Your Father created you wholly without sin, wholly without pain and wholly without suffering of any kind. If you deny Him you bring sin, pain and suffering into your own mind because of the power He gave it. Your mind is capable of creating worlds, but it can also deny what it creates because it is free.*

T177.3/191.9

# Teacher of God

Anyone who chooses to be a Teacher of God can make that choice. The desire to reflect God and Christ in his/her life has come upon them. When they are ready, the student appears; when the student is ready, the teacher appears. The teacher learns from the student and vice versa. They come together for mutual healing.

*A teacher of God is anyone who chooses to be one. His qualifications consist solely in this; somehow, somewhere he has made a deliberate choice in which he did not see his interests as apart from someone else's. Once he has done that, his road is established and his direction is sure. A light has entered the darkness. It may be a single light, but that is enough. He has entered an agreement with God even if he does not yet believe in Him. He has become a bringer of salvation. He has become a teacher of God.*

TM3.1/3.1

*The teachers of God have no set teaching level. Each teaching-learning situation involves a different relationship at the beginning, although the ultimate goal is always the same; to make of the relationship a holy relationship, in which both can look upon the Son of God as sinless. There is no one from whom a teacher of God cannot learn, so there is no one whom he cannot teach.*

TM6.1/7.1

*The teachers of God have trust in the world, because they have learned it is not governed by the laws the world made up. It is governed by a power that is in them but not of them. It is this power that keeps all things safe. It is through this power that the teachers of God look on a forgiven world.*

TM8.3/9.1

# Time

Time is an illusion. The easiest way to disconnect from Spirit is to be guilty about actions in the past or to fear what unknown horrors may be in the future. Now is the only time that matters, as yesterday is history and tomorrow is only a possibility. Who can drive a car appropriately while looking on the rearview mirror? Yesterday is gone. You can't change it. Live in the precious "now" moment when all things are possible.

*Ultimately, space is as meaningless as time. Both are merely beliefs.*

T11.3/14.3

*Time itself is your choice. If you would remember eternity, you must look only on the eternal. If you allow yourself to become preoccupied with the temporal, you are living in time . . . time and eternity cannot both be real, because they contradict each other. If you will accept only what is timeless as real, you will begin to understand eternity and make it yours.*

T178.4/192.14

*The cloud that obscures God's Son to you **is** the past . . . The miracle enables you to see your brother without his past, and so perceive him as born again. His errors are all past, and by perceiving him without them you are releasing him. And since his past is yours, you share in this release.*

T234.0 & .1/251.4 & .5

*Yet every instant can you be reborn, and given life again.*

T505.3/543.7

. . . *Now is the closest approximation of eternity that this world offers.*

T230.0/246, 7

*Each day, each hour and minute, even each second, you are deciding between the crucifixion and the resurrection; between the ego and the Holy Spirit.*

T255.4/275.4

# Wishes

If wishes were horses...

*Wishes are not facts. To wish is to imply that willing is not sufficient. Yet no one in his right mind believes that what is wished is as real as what is willed.*

T44.2/49.11

*It is, then, only your wish to change reality that is fearful, because by your wish you think you have accomplished what you wish. This strange position, in a sense, acknowledges your power. Yet by distorting it and devoting it to "evil," it also makes it unreal. You cannot be faithful to two masters who ask conflicting things of you. What you use in fantasy you deny to truth. Yet what you give to truth to use for you is safe from fantasy.*

T327.2/351.2

*The wish to see calls down the grace of God upon your eyes, and brings the gift of light that makes sight possible.*

T492.4/529.3

# The World

This world, including your body and all events in the world, is only a teaching device to learn the way home to God. All events are neutral and for your greater good, no matter how terrible they seem to be. You are responsible for your experiences. There is no one to blame, especially not yourself. Be thankful for them as opportunities to grow. The world is insane—not to be taken seriously. See above the horrors of this world to the Truth of God behind it.

*The real purpose of this world is to use it to correct your unbelief.*

T11.4/14.4

*Sit quietly and look upon the world you see, and tell yourself: "The real world is not like this. It has no buildings and there are no streets where people walk alone and separate." ...The world you see must be denied, for sight of it is costing you a different kind of vision.* **You cannot see both worlds,** *for each of them involves a different kind of seeing, and depends on what you cherish.*

T236.3 & .4/254.1 & .2

*You have been wrong about the world because you have misjudged yourself. From such a twisted reference point, what could you see? All seeing starts with the perceiver, who judges what is true and what is false. And what he judges false he does not see.*

T237.1/254–5

*There is a light that this world cannot give. Yet you can give it, as it was given you. And as you give it, it shines forth to call you from the world and follow it. For this light will attract you as nothing in this world can do.*

*And you will lay aside the world and find another. This other world is bright with love which you have given it. And here will everything remind you of your Father and His Holy Son. Light is unlimited, and spreads across this world in quiet joy.*

T235.4/253.11

*The world as you perceive it cannot have been created by the Father, for the world is not as you see it. God created only the eternal, and everything you see is perishable.*

T194.4/210.2

# Glossary

Some often used terms and principles are as follows:

- ➤ **Blasphemy** – You commit blasphemy when you "play small." When you have low self-esteem, you do not love yourself with the Love that God has for you. Because God created you, when you don't see yourself the way He sees you, you demean Him.

- ➤ **Brotherhood** – A brother's cry of rage is merely a call for a response of love. What you see in your brother is what you see in yourself and what you strengthen in yourself. Your brother is your teacher and your reflection.

- ➤ **Creation** – occurred when God extended Himself to you. You are a divine expression of God in whom He is well pleased.

- ➤ **Defenselessness** – Your defenses and reactions attract attack. When you become defenseless and at peace, those who would attack you find some other outlet for their activities and you remain at peace.

- ➤ **Ego** – a part of your thought system that tries to separate you from God; it is not real. You only need to understand how it operates in your life, to be aware of its voice in your ear, to take away its power. "Edging God Out."

- ➤ **Forgiveness** – seeing with a new perception and realizing that nothing ever truly happened that needs to be forgiven.

- ➤ **Grandeur vs. grandiosity** – Grandeur is of God, while grandiosity is of the ego. When you claim your part of God's Kingdom, you recognize your grandness, or your grandeur. Grandiosity is delusional.

- ➤ **Grace** – Unmerited assistance given man for his regeneration or sanctification.

> **Healing** – Healing results and peace is experienced as you become aware that your spiritual self cannot be sick and that your physical self need not be sick. Your brothers everywhere are blessed by your healing and you are blessed by any healing anywhere.

> **Holiness** – wholeness, the awareness of your oneness with God. Holiness and wholeness are the same—nothing missing and nothing lacking. God and you are one; you are perfect, whole, and complete.

> **Illusions** – what you see with the eyes of the body and are colored by your past history, while Truth and Knowledge are what you see with the eyes of the Spirit.

> **Judgment** – only God can judge truly. When you are judging, you are in hell. When you are forgiving, you are in Heaven.

> **Love** – is all there truly is. Giving love strengthens it in yourself. Love is the answer to all meaningful questions.

> **Miracles** – are natural and should occur without strain—if they are not occurring, something is wrong. A miracle is a new way of looking at something or someone, and is not necessarily an event in the physical world. It is a parting of the clouds that hide the truth. Miracles are never lost or wasted and may touch many people and many situations of which you may never be aware.

> **Salvation** – is the replacing of ego-thoughts of conflict with thoughts of peace; it results in healing.

> **Separation** – You are not, nor ever could be, separated from God. The ego would have you believe that you are separated, small, afraid, and alone—like a child hidden underneath the covers. Return to Love! Dismiss the ego and its insanity for it leads nowhere.

> **Specialness** – If you consider yourself as a special case, to be treated differently because you have excuses for having the problems that you have, then this comes under the category of specialness, as defined in the Course.

> **This World** – including your body and all events in the world, is only a teaching device to learn the way home to

God. All events are neutral and for your greater good, no matter how terrible they seem to be. You are responsible for your experiences. There is no one to blame, not even you. Be thankful for them as opportunities to grow. The world is insane—not to be taken seriously. See above the horrors of this world to the Truth of God behind it.

➤ **Time** – Now is the only time that matters, as yesterday is history and tomorrow is only a possibility.

# About the Author

I have been studying metaphysical principles and facilitating study groups in *A Course in Miracles* for close to twenty years. This book is taken from my teaching notes and material that has inspired me through the years. I am an author, poet, and artist. My poetry is sprinkled throughout this document. I wrote, printed, published, and distributed my first book, *A Course in Miracles in a Nutshell* in 1997. This volume is a new, expanded Second Edition, and it is now the first in a trilogy of *"Nutshell"* volumes, all available now. The other two books are:

*A Course in Miracles in a Nutshell Book Two: Inspirational Messages from the Heart*

(ISBN 0-9777219-1-4, $14.00, Transformation Publications, Mesa AZ) and

*A Course in Miracles in a Nutshell Book Three: More Inspirational Messages from the Heart*

(ISBN 0-9777219-2-2, $14.00, Transformation Publications, Mesa AZ)

All of my books are available in bookstores, at many online bookstores such as Amazon.com, and direct from my personal website, http://www.budmorris.com.

My goal in life is to remember more of my spiritual truth each day and to teach that truth to everyone I meet; i.e., to unconditionally love everyone I encounter and to help heal the insanity of this world through that unconditional love. I seek each day to be continually practicing the Presence of God and to pray unceasingly, at the same time carrying on a life filled with activities.

Printed in the United States
76417LV00004B/211-213

9 780977 721900